The RESILIENT SUPERVISOR

Leadership Skills for Supervisors of High-Impact Organizations

DR. DE HICKS

President and CEO
RMC Group of Companies
Founder of the *Archimedes Experiment*

Copyright © 2019 by De Hicks
All rights reserved.

Cover design by Allan Ytac
Interior design by Allan Ytac
Copy Editor: Rebecca B. Hayes www.thewritingqueen.com

ISBN-13: 978-1-0915-9304-6

No part of this book may be reproduced or transmitted in any form or by any means, electronic or mechanical, including photocopying, recording, or b any infomation storage and retrieval system, without permission in writing from the author.

Published by RMC Group of Companies and The Archimedes Experiment

Table of Contents

Preface 1

Introduction 5
   What is a High-Impact Organization? 5
   Is this Book for You? 6
   How to Use this Book. 7

Chapter 1: Why You Work--Purpose as the Ultimate Point
   of Leverage 9
   The Ultimate Point of Leverage 10
   Effective Supervisors Care 11
   Two Forms of Power. 12
   Point of Leverage 13
   Your Team Deserves Good Supervision 13
   Point of Leverage 14

Chapter 2: One of Our Most Significant Relationships 15
   Point of Leverage 16
   You Have One Job 16
   Point of Leverage 17
   One Job, Three Roles. 17
   Point of Leverage 20

Chapter 3: Considering Becoming a Supervisor? 23

Chapter 4: Transitioning to Supervisor--The Five Rs 27
   A Change in Your Role 28
   A Change in the Rules of Engagement 29

A Change in Relationships 31
A Change in Resources 32
A Change in Responsibilities 33
Point of Leverage 33

Chapter 5: Bring your Brain to Work--
The Power of Assumptions 35
    "Just Enough" Focus and Attention 37
    Point of Leverage 40
    Upgrading Our Mental Models and Assumptions 41
    Think Correctly about Work 42
    Grandmother, Counselor, Dispatcher 42
    Point of Leverage 43

Chapter 6: Listen to Mental Models--
The Dog Whistle of Leadership 45
    Conflict is an Invitation to Check My Assumptions 46
    Let's Review: Filling in the Blanks Correctly 46
    Our Assumptions Weren't Built in a Day 48
    Invisible Operating Systems of our Assumptions 49
    Our Brain's Superpower: Pattern Recognition 50
    The Black Hole of Grouchiness 52

Chapter 7: Insight from Behavioral Economics 53
    The Delicate Art of Changing Precious Mental Models 54
    Point of Leverage 57

Chapter 8: Our Greatest Challenge:
Overcoming Our Own Psychology 59
    Fundamental One: Focus-- o This, and You Won't Go Crazy 59
    Fundamental Two: Stewardship of Time--Surprise! You Will

    Never Have Enough Time 60
    Fundamental Three: Decision Making and Decision Fatigue 61
    Fundamental Four: Worry is Fear on Simmer--What are You
    Worried About? 62
    Fundamental Five: Focus on Performance 62

Chapter 9: Connectivity's Dark Side and the Impact on Supervisors.. 65
    More About Networks 66
    The Bigger Picture 67
    Adjustment Disorders and Other Unintended Consequences of
    Connectivity 69
    Faster AND Better 71
    The Often-Misunderstood Impact of Connectivity 71
    Outsourcing Responsibility and Making Three Choices....... 72
    Practice Responsibility 73
    Choice is an Amazing Thing 74

Chapter 10: Culture--How It Really Works Around Here....... 77
    Do You Have Any Spam Cans? 79
    The Keepers of the Culture........................... 80
    Norms are Always Twins 81
    Point of Leverage 82

Chapter 11: Understanding and Communicating the WHY 83
    The Purpose of the Supervisory Relationship 84
    The Challenge of Consistency 85
    The *So That* Model................................. 87
    Clarify the *Why* Behind the *What* 88
    Point of Leverage 90

Chapter 12: Conflict--The Great Mirror 91
    Managing Conflict 92

Chapter 13: Creating and Leading within a Results-Oriented Work Environment 97

Chapter 14: This is Changing. This is Not Changing. 101
    Point of Leverage 104

Chapter 15: The Unintended Consequences of Venting 105

Chapter 16: Creating a One Call, One Click, One Conversation Culture. 111
    Three Types of Communication 113

Chapter 17: Performance Standards are the Resilient Supervisor's Best Friend. 115
    Ten Characteristics of Clear Performance Standards 116

Chapter 18: Performance Management Tools 119
    Performance Management Tool 1: The Power of Expectations .. 119
    Nod and Smile 121
    Written Expectations 122
    Performance Management Tool 2: Breaking the Bermuda Triangle of Communication 125
    Performance Management Tool 3: What? What? What? ... 129
    Point of Leverage 130
    Performance Management Tool 4: The SLY Model 130
    Leo and Linda 133
    Performance Management Tool 5: The Skill of Tipping 135
    Performance Management Tool 6: The OIC Model 136
    Performance Management Tool 7: The Myth of the Right Time ... 140

  Look in the Mirror 144

Chapter 19: Your Calendar is Your Most Powerful Tool **145**
  The Principle of One. 146

Chapter 20: He's NOT a Good Engineer **151**

Chapter 21: Tips for Becoming and Remaining a Resilient Supervisor (and a Healthy Team Member) **157**
  Some People Adapt and Stay Healthy 159
  The Disciplines of Healthy High-Impact Supervisors 160

Chapter 22: Time to Multiply--Erickson's Stages of Life and the Lessons for Supervisory Leaders **163**

Chapter 23: A Bias for Action. **167**
  Point of Leverage 173
  Minimize the Change: Small Steps, Large Results. 173

Chapter 24: Conclusion. **175**

Chapter 25: The Short List of Resilient Supervisor Skills **177**

About the Author **181**

INDEX **183**

About the Archimedes Experiment **188**

Preface

High Impact organizations have been responsible for most of the monumental shifts in human history. From war to Wonder Bread, from archery to AirPods, High-Impact organizations, large and small, have created or accelerated every grand pivot throughout time. Our study and experience with High-Impact organizations and their teams have yielded a river of gold for us. It is worth sharing with you.

All High-Impact organizations are comprised of small groups of people focused on achieving substantial results. These small groups are the engines of impact.

We are social creatures and throughout history have arranged ourselves into small groups that provide everything from protection to sense of personhood. Much of what we understand of ourselves, other people, our work and world comes from these groups.

In modern history, some of these groups have become exceptionally organized, focusing on changing unsolvable problems into expansive opportunities. Groups create.

And some groups create so rapidly that other groups emerge solely to keep track of, market and manage the implementation of innovations.

Now groups are more connected than at any time in human history. Time and space between groups and their ideas have all but vanished.

Where *disconnected* was the default throughout human history, now *connected* is the default. Connectivity has become the norm, resulting in acceleration of the creative arch.

Some groups have achieved outsized impact on markets, subcultures, the economy, and society. These groups, large and small, we call "High-Impact groups." When branded, organized, focused and arranged with other such groups, we get "High-Impact organizations."

My personal interest in these High-Impact organizations and their subgroups of High-Impact teams arose in early adolescence when I noticed with curiosity that some groups, whether families, small companies, schools or sports teams, far outpaced the effectiveness of others. The dairy farm to the south of us was three times more profitable than the one to the north, even with similar resources and history. The high school football team in the neighboring school district beat my alma mater soundly season after season. Both schools drew from the same demographic and were the same size.

In the fall of my fourth-grade year of elementary school, the Hungry Onion opened for business on the corner of South Main and East Water Tower Lane. On the other side of the street, three months later, Jack's Jumbo Burgers began operations. The two fast-food restaurants had similar menus and price points, similar curb appeal and targeted the same markets. Jack's closed its doors within three years. The Hungry Onion is still open (and thriving) nearly 50 years later.

Why? Why do some groups, whether formed as teams, Special Forces, or businesses, thrive while others falter? This is, of course, a simple question with subtle and complex answers.

In this book, I will highlight one of the most common reasons why groups succeed: highly effective middle leadership.

I will also attempt to make sense of over 30 years of research into what makes a middle leader in High-Impact organizations effective. What are the skills, disciplines, and assumptions of successful middle leaders that set them apart from the ones we all whisper about in the break room?

PREFACE

Most often, those middle leaders hold supervisory positions. Therefore, throughout this book, I will unpack the competencies, mental models and skills consistently demonstrated by those who hold supervisory (whether official or not) positions.

High-Impact organizations all have highly effective middle leaders in supervisory positions. And those highly effective supervisors often do the same things, demonstrate similar competencies, practice the same disciplines and view themselves and their jobs from the same mental models. Their skills were learned rather than genetically imposed. Therefore, we can learn them as well.

This book is about those skills and how to practice them.

Introduction

You've accepted the promotion to become a Supervisor. You know this is an important role. You are now one of the most significant people in your High- Impact organization. It felt like a promotion, a natural next step in your career, but it did not take long to realize that this is a very different job than the one you had.

> *Of all the meaningful relationships we have in our lives, our Supervisory relationship is one of the most significant.*

What is a High-Impact Organization?

High-Impact organizations are unlike other human enterprises. Whether small or large, they stand out in history because they create opportunities, markets and even movements where little existed before. Whether public or private, High-Impact organizations lead while others follow. They innovate and often implement in untested environments. They are intensely mission-focused and fiercely forward-looking. Their velocity of work is double or triple that of their nearest competitors or contemporaries. Their teams communicate ten times as much as other moderately performing organizations.

They are the Paper of Record in the news industry; they are the

Special Forces in the military; they are the Mayo Clinic of teaching hospitals; they are the Tesla of automotive companies; they are the Phoenix Fire Department of emergency services; they are the Amazon of the consumer experience; they are the Acton Academies of education.

High-Impact organizations are intensely focused on a leveraged mission that accomplishes layered results. They have an inspiring vision, clear goals, skilled and humble leadership and philosophy of finance that supports continual learning throughout the enterprise.

High-Impact organizations, whether staffed by 6 or 60,000 people, obsessively communicate plans, resolve conflict on the fly and crave continual improvement.

High-Impact organizations create intentional rather than accidental cultures. They attract high-performing individuals and structure everything they do around small teams.

Finally, High-Impact organizations are result oriented. They achieve daily, weekly and monthly results. They pivot when results are delayed or derailed and celebrate every achievement, large or small.

High-Impact organizations create the future.[1]

Is this Book for You?

If you are a Supervisor in a High-Impact organization, leading a High-Impact team, this book is for you. If you are thinking of becoming a Supervisor, supervise just one other person or lead a group of Supervisors, this book is for you. If you have been surprised by how challenging the job is, this book is for you.

If you are looking for proven principles and effective, behavior-based approaches to complex challenges, you will appreciate this book. While this book describes Resilient Supervisors as leaders in a High-Impact

---

[1] High-Impact organizations, while not the norm, can be found in almost every industry and profession. They get results over and over. They are not accidentally excellent, but intentionally so. They appear ruthless from the outside but inclusive and inspiring from within.

organization, the perspectives and tools, called **Points of Leverage**, can be used in almost any supervisory setting.

If you think of yourself as a leader, the concepts of connectivity, workplace culture, assumptions, performance management, and mental models will be especially helpful.

I have worked to make the ideas in this book direct and memorable. While there are a few case studies or short stories, they do not occupy many pages as I am sure you have personal illustrations that will readily come to mind.

How to Use this Book

This book is part of **The Archimedes Experiment®**. Archimedes of Syracuse, a fourth-century Greek mathematician, described the power of leverage in his riveting page-turner "On the Equilibrium of Planes." He wrote, "Give me a lever, a fulcrum and a place to stand, and I will move the earth."[2] An intriguing figure in history, Archimedes was credited with an array of original thought that lives on today.[3]

The concepts shared here and in my other books in this series are themselves highly leveraged. Small amounts of effort applied consistently at the right place and in the proper manner will yield outsized results. I think of this effort as an experiment since we must discover the right ways and points in time to apply leveraged skills.

Look for **Point of Leverage** segments throughout this book.

---

2   As quoted by Pappus of Alexandria, *Synagoge, Book VIII*, c. AD 340; also found in *Chiliades* (12th century) by John Tzetzes, II.130. Not that you have access to a copy of this. I'm a footnote reader so I will include all manner of minutia throughout the book that will dramatically increase the time it takes to read. Have fun.

3   Archimedes of Syracuse (d: c 212) was credited with describing the power of leverage, the calculation of Pi, the law of buoyancy, the principles of flotation and displacement, early versions of calculus, the derived formulas of the surface area of a sphere and of a sphere's volume, the first description of the concept of infinity and more. He created the Archimedes Screw, still in use in many applications today, and the odometer. He even invented the Claw of Archimedes. Look it up.

They are practical applications of the ideas I describe. They are simple behavioral changes that yield weighty results.

Also look for **The Resilient Supervisor: Skill #1** (etc.) throughout this book. They are short reminders of the practical skills practiced by Supervisors who have been effective over a long period. Emulate them by practicing these skills, and you will be exceptionally resilient.

Other books, blog posts, and videos in **The Archimedes Experience**® are being created regularly. Look for them at ArchimedesExperiment.com and at **The De Hicks Podcast** © available on iTunes ® and other platforms.

The chapters that follow are short and can be scanned. Each section can stand alone. The order in which you read is not essential. Scan the Table of Contents and pick what interests you. Read that first. Put the book down and come back to it when your interest in another theme piques. `

This book was also designed to be helpful in Supervisory training programs. Arrange the chapters to fit the challenges your Supervisory team faces, read them in advance of your classes or meetings and discuss the **Points of Leverage** as they relate to your work.

Chapter 1:

Why You Work--Purpose as the Ultimate Point of Leverage

The alarm sounds at 5:00 a.m. It's the sixth day of work in a row. Seven hours of sleep feels like four. *Why am I doing this? Is it for the money? Or the glory?* Probably not enough of either. *Maybe it's the fame.*

Think about it: Why do you work? Don't read much further before you answer the question.

Why are you in this specific job? Your first thought, formed in an instant, is probably the primary reason.

> *Don't read on until you are clear about the reasons you are in this job.*

Do you work to eat? Do you work to buy fun things? Or to have security? Do you work for other reasons and putting food on the table is a helpful and necessary benefit? Do you work at this job because you don't see any other choices? Clarifying why you work, and why you work at *this* job, is critical. If you are not clear about this, you will not be as resilient as you need to be. And you'll work for other people's purposes.

But if you are clear about why you are in *this* job, and if it's beyond money, and if it's worth it to you (worth getting out of bed even on cold, dark days), then you are free. Then you no longer work for money or for the boss or the company but for a purpose.

There. Master this and everything else makes more sense.

When we study the most effective and resilient leaders at every level, we find that they are clear about why they choose to do their particular job. And their "why" transcends a paycheck. Their purpose in the position makes the daily and weekly challenges worth surmounting. They *choose* to do this job. They do not feel trapped. They are free. Free leaders are a force of nature.

> **The Resilient Supervisor Skill #1: Figure out why you work.**

The Ultimate Point of Leverage

Two Questions: Answer them quickly. Don't overthink.

First: When, in the last few weeks, have you felt delighted with something you accomplished (as an individual or as part of a group) at work?

Second: (Stop… don't answer this until you've responded to the first question.) Why do you work? Don't overthink the question.

Third: (Stop… don't answer this until you've responded to the second question.) Why THIS job? You have a choice. Why this specific job?

Therefore, I *choose* to work at this job so that _____.

If, after thinking about why you do this job, you concluded that your purpose is entirely to achieve financial security, change jobs. Make a plan. Take the first step to implement the plan. Today. It may take a few months (or more) to achieve the plan but get started today. The job you are in now will only get harder. There isn't enough money in the budget to compensate for the increased complexity you will see.

We are at a time when there are more jobs than people to fill them, especially jobs that require your competencies. If you are in it only for the money, get creative, get courageous and get out. Two years from now, you will thank me. And so will your team.

If, however, you are in this job as a leader because it is precisely where you need and want to be, you will have the endurance to learn the skills, practice them until they become second-nature and thrive.

Effective Supervisors Care

When we ask why people choose to be Supervisors, the same basic answers emerge. Effective Supervisors and leaders care. They all said they do the work because they genuinely care.

Resilient Supervisors are thoughtful in deciding what to care about. They care about the individual's effectiveness more than they care about feelings. They care about the team more than the individual, about the mission more than themselves and about the mission and impact more than systems or structures.

They care about the results. Effective leaders in Supervisory roles are results oriented. They know what results must be achieved. They know how to measure and use rules and tools to accomplish meaningful results.

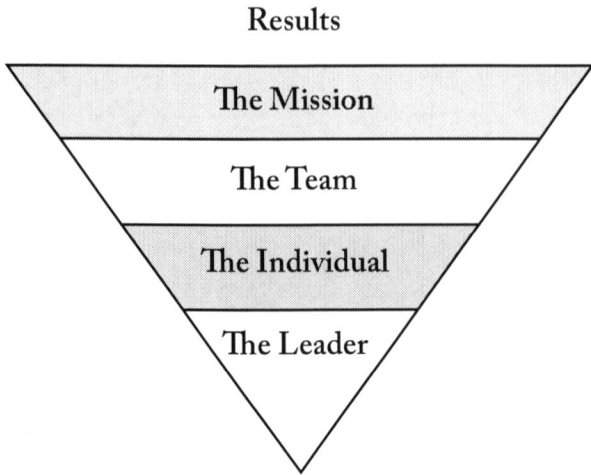

Two Forms of Power

The leader with Supervisory responsibility fills a powerful position. This power is essential. It takes on two forms: First, the Supervisor can decide. Second, he has the power to explain what things mean and how they work.

The latter is the more significant source of power. All effective Supervisors, therefore, are compulsive about explaining what things mean and about getting their team members to see and understand the *why* behind every decision. They regularly talk about what decisions and events mean. They never let an incorrect interpretation of an event go unanswered.

> *Explaining correctly what things mean is the most significant source of power at the leader's disposal.*

Point of Leverage

Listen carefully this week for opportunities to clarify what things mean. Take three opportunities and insert yourself into the conversation. Directly challenge incorrect assumptions about what something means by saying, "No, you are incorrect. It does not mean that. It means this." You do not need to engage in a debate or slowly, gently persuade. Simply speak up. *Never let an incorrect assumption go unchallenged.*

> **The Resilient Supervisor Skill #2: All effective Supervisors are compulsive about explaining what things mean and about getting their team members to see and understand the why behind every decision. They regularly talk about what decisions and events mean. They never let an incorrect interpretation of an event go unanswered.**

Your Team Deserves Good Supervision

The people you supervise deserve a leader who cares about them, about the mission of the organization and about continual improvement.

In my experience, the most effective and resilient Supervisors are driven by the desire to see other people perform at their highest levels; they are compelled to see teams and individuals grow and thrive; they are motivated to see important results. They care about the mission of the organization or enterprise and get a thrill out of developing others. They care about the joy that comes when people they supervise grow. Does this describe you?

Point of Leverage

Dream of doing another job. Really think about it. Imagine what it would be like. Is it better than the one you have now? If so, reach out to two people who do that job. Set up a phone call and ask them to describe the position. Go deep. Ask them to be direct and blunt about the job. Then think about your role as a Supervisor. What parts do you love? What parts would you miss? Be realistic.

Now take action: If your job as Supervisor wins out, double down on the parts of your job you love. Do work you are proud of. Nothing reinvigorates like excellence.

Chapter 2:

One of Our Most Significant Relationships

As I wrote before, the Supervisory relationship is one of the most significant ones working people have. It is likely one of the most talked about ones as well. The Supervisor has a massive impact on the well-being of the team. Think of the most effective Supervisors you have had in your career so far. Now think of the least effective Supervisors you have had. In both categories, the people who came to mind were subjects of conversation over dinner and drinks with friends and family. The ineffective Supervisor is the source of early morning anxiety and one-sided post-work rants in the car on your way home. The effective ones are a resource and welcome additions to the breakroom and after-work parties.

Over the years, I have asked many frustrated employees what they would like their ineffective Supervisor to change and have been struck by the simplicity of their lists. They often complain about being kept out of the loop, being mistreated, about being misunderstood. Their suggested solutions are straightforward:

» Tell me what they expect and stick to it;
» listen to my ideas for improvement;

- » flex with me (often preceded with a "Good God! Just flex a little.");
- » remember that rules are tools and change them when they don't work anymore;
- » tell me why;
- » say please and thank you;
- » give me regular feedback about my performance.

By far the most impassioned complaints have to do with not dealing with poor performers on the team and shifting work from slackers to stars as a way of compensating for lousy job from underperformers.

Point of Leverage

Take Stock. How are you doing with each of these expectations?
1. I keep my team, as a group and as individuals, in the loop.
2. I am just in my decisions and explain my rationale.
3. I work hard to understand what it's really like to do their jobs.
4. I clarify my expectations, including the why regularly.
5. I solicit ideas for improvement.
6. I am results oriented and clarify the results I expect.
7. I am flexible if the results are achieved.
8. I say "Please."
9. I say "Thank you," and I mean it.
10. I give regular, timely, behavior-focused feedback.
11. I quickly address poor performance.

You Have One Job

Your role as a Supervisor, while robust and impactful, is quite simple. You have one job: Performance Improvement. The Supervisory relationship exists for that one purpose.

It is not about therapy, although challenging and meaningful work is therapeutic. It does not exist for friendship, although friendly Supervisors are much more effective than unfriendly ones. It does not exist for unconditional family-style love, although Supervisors who genuinely care about people are much more effective than those who do not. The Supervisory role does not exist to make people happy, although happiness usually results from meaningful work done well.

As a Supervisor, you are not a detective. You are not a sister, brother or uncle. You are not a butler or barista. You are not a psychologist, even though knowing what really matters to your team members is essential. Your job is about one thing: better performance. Better performance for the team and for the individual.

Therefore, all effective Supervisors are crystal clear about the results their team and organization are trying to accomplish. They know what a good job looks like and they consistently challenge people to achieve at a higher level. All of them. All the time.

Point of Leverage

1. Identify one of the people or job types you supervise.
2. Concisely describe the top three elements of a good job. Identify what a good job looks like by using behavioral terms and the "this, not that" model.
3. Compare each of the people you supervise (who have this specific job) to this description of a good job.
4. What did you discover?

One Job, Three Roles

In achieving better performance, effective Supervisors play three roles. They become a compass, a window, and a mirror. To be a compass, he knows the direction his team needs to go and frequently points it out. As a window, the Supervisor frames and re-frames every change so that it is understood in its proper context. As a mirror, he accurately reflects the behavior of the individual and the team.

Acting as a compass, the effective Supervisor reminds the team, for example, about its mission and about those who benefit from accomplishment.

Acting as a window, she reframes a 10-hour day full of annoying distractions as "the dues we pay to stay in the game."

ONE OF OUR MOST SIGNIFICANT RELATIONSHIPS

Acting as a mirror, the sharp Supervisor privately and respectfully points out the team member's inappropriate behavior saying, "You have complained loudly after each meeting today." No more words are necessary.

Most Supervisors feel the urge to just… keep… talking… and… talking… to justify their observation. But when playing the role of the mirror, fewer words are better.

All three roles are essential. However, playing the role of the mirror is the most difficult. It is easy to "go internal" with someone by talking with them about their motivations or thoughts in an attempt to unravel the Gordian knot of their psychology.

"I'm sure you are tired today and came from a negative, un-nurturing family setting fraught with peril, but you sound abrupt and rude when replying to people." Avoid the urge to play psychologist or priest.

Mirrors (except for the manipulative Mirror on the Wall of *Snow White* fame) only reflect what is on the outside. A good mirror reflects "You have spinach in your teeth" and not "You are an unaware slob who obviously likes his spinach salad way too much." A good mirror only helps the team member see her behavior.

When coupled with clear expectations rooted in values, the mirror is the most influential role you play.

How long should you wait before reflecting behavior back to the individual? Minutes are better than hours. As soon as you can get a moment to be a mirror, take it. Do not wait for a pattern to develop over several hours or days. Do it now, as long as it is a quiet and private conversation. If you wait for patterns to emerge, you will only see the behavior you are looking for and exaggerate its overall significance. You will also create distrust as the employee wonders (silently at first) why you did not address it earlier and what else you are keeping track of only to reveal later.

> *The most effective and resilient Supervisors are clear about expectations, direct in their communication style, consistently kind and respectful in their approach, relentless about follow-up and results oriented. They experience their greatest joy when their team does well.*

As a Supervisor, setting clear and high expectations is your most important work. Expectations need to be specific, behavioral and mostly measurable. They need to be clearly anchored to the underlying value that created them.

"I expect that you arrive early enough before your shift to be calm and prepared and understand what the last hour of the previous shift was like so that 1.) team members can end their shift on time and 2.) customers do not have to wait."

Point of Leverage

Think about a member of your Team with whom you've been a little frustrated. It's likely you have given your frustration with his performance a psychological or an internal motivation label. Try to identify the behavior you see and describe the action you want instead.

Instead of "bad attitude," what do you see behaviorally that makes you think he has a bad attitude? Reflect that.

Instead of "doesn't care," what do you see behaviorally that makes you think she doesn't care? Reflect that.

If the behavior (arriving late, terse responses, poor spelling, arguing) is a problem, merely point it out and ask that it be changed.

> **Resilient Supervisory Skill #3: Practice being a Compass, a Window, and a Mirror.**

Chapter 3:

Considering Becoming a Supervisor?

There are few people on the planet who do what you do. Smaller still is the number of people who are resilient and exceptional at this job over the long haul. Find them. Befriend them. Ask them how they do it.

The job can be mentally and physically draining. It takes a toll that is not readily evident. Look around at Supervisors who have been doing it for more than a couple of years. Most of them show signs of mental and physical fatigue, even after returning from several days off.

But not all of them. A few are genuinely resilient and seem as fresh as the day they took the job. Even after years, their humor is sharp, they are energetic and embrace change. They have much to teach the newer Supervisor and will usually share willingly if asked.

So ask them how they did it. Ask them what they regularly do to remain engaged. At first, they will say it's in the genes, or it's just common sense, or they don't really know. But stick with it. Ask very practical and simple questions and get them talking. We've done it with hundreds of Supervisors over the years. Much of what I've written here is the direct result of those conversations and observations.

One of the themes they all mention is the relationship they have with other Supervisors. They work at developing healthy, collaborative relationships with others in Supervisory positions in their organization. They communicate regularly and overcome schedule complexities, to do so. They avoid triangulation and engage with one another about supervisory challenges.

Your relationship with the other Supervisors in your own organization is a crucial one. As we have participated in the search, interview and hiring process for nearly two hundred Supervisory positions, one of the most important qualities we look for in a candidate is the potential fit with the current Supervisory team.

Since most Supervisory teams need to grow in some way, we look for at least the following qualities:

- » Will she be able to transition from her current role into a Supervisory role without leaving a wreck behind?
- » Can she communicate and problem solve with strong personalities on the Supervisory team?
- » Will she work hard at learning her new role?
- » Will she be able to add a perspective to the Supervisory team that it lacks?
- » Will she address Supervisory team inconsistencies?
- » Will she put the needs of the team above her own?

If you are considering applying for a Supervisory position, your current work relationships will change. Therefore, think about these questions:

- » What impact will the new position have on my strongest relationships (at home and at work)?
- » What impact will the schedule have?
- » Consider the most forceful personality on the Supervisory team and think about how you will handle conflict with him or her.
- » The Supervisory team has a Supervisor. Will you be able to take direction from her?

Turning the intensity of the job off at the end of a day is essential to your long-term vitality. While challenging for some employees, it is much more challenging for Supervisors. Do you have the disciplines in place that allow you to entirely focus on other things outside of work and only occasionally bring work home with you? Can you support and reinforce policies, rules, and approaches with which you disagree? Can you work to change those rules (an excruciatingly slow process in most organizations) even while you support them?

As a Supervisor promoted from within the ranks, you will be asking coworkers to change behaviors that you had just weeks ago. Can you humbly do that? If you have an excellent Supervisor now, it is probable he is supportive and expresses appreciation, even thanks you, for a job well done. As a Supervisor, you will likely go months at a time without ever hearing a simple "Thank You." Are you okay with that?

As a front-line employee, you could distance yourself from people you didn't like. As a Supervisor, you will not have that luxury. In fact, there will be times when your days will be consumed with interactions with people that you would not have coffee with under any circumstances. Are you ready to serve them and keep your preferences out of view?

Finally, before becoming a Supervisor, your performance was YOUR performance. You succeeded or failed, but it was about you. Now as a Supervisor, your performance is measured mainly by the performance of others. Are you good at giving others credit when 90% of the effort was yours?

If all these dynamics pale in comparison to the thrill of seeing a team perform at higher and higher levels, if they are insignificant compared to the satisfaction that comes from seeing a struggling employee turn her performance around and thrive, then you might be ready to begin the new job as a Supervisor.

Chapter 4:

Transitioning to Supervisor--The Five Rs

Many Supervisory positions are filled by experienced employees with proven competencies and skills commensurate with the demands of a front-line job. This often means that newly promoted Supervisors will lead people who were their peers just a few days ago. This transition can be surprisingly complex. It can have unexpected impacts on schedules, finances, and friendships.

Now that you have taken on the role of a leader, you will experience a change in the **Five Rs of Leadership**: a change in your **Role** means a change in the **Rules** of Engagement, a change in **Relationships**, a change in access to **Resources** and a change in **Responsibilities**. Change one of the **Rs** and the others also change.

This transition is not experienced all at once. It can happen slowly as situations prompt awareness that "something is different." A walk down the hallway past animated conversations results in abrupt posture changes or blunted sentences. A casual stroll into the breakroom to refresh your coffee results in a barely noticeable increase in formality from others seated having lunch. A new monitor at your desk yields a "must be nice" snark from your friend. Your Thursday morning breakfast

tradition with two of your eight co-workers seems oddly exclusive now.
Something has changed, and everyone feels it.

A Change in Your Role

Altering your Role from experienced peer to Supervisor of a group of peers means your work has changed. You are starting over. The essence of the job itself is now different. It doesn't take long to realize that this promotion was not a natural step; it is a change in positions.

As a front-line employee, you were clear what a good job looked like. Your performance was mainly *your* performance. Now your effectiveness is mostly dependent on other people's performance. This change is profound.

> *If the new Supervisor does not come to terms with this change in focus, she will likely still try to find personal reward in doing the work of the front-line team member. This means she will feel the need to be as good as, or better than, the front-line team members. The result is unnecessary competition and a vacancy in the duties required of the Supervisor.*

If you've been a Supervisor for even a few months, you have come to understand that your transition from front-line employee to Supervisor was not a natural, linear one. It didn't take long to realize this. The new **Role** meant all the other **Rs** were new too. The change in your **Role** triggered a cascade of changes in the **Rules** of Engagement, in your **Relationships**, in your access to **Resources** and in your specific **Responsibilities**.

Watching this transition from afar, or seeing it in an org-chart, may have given you the idea that it would be a simple progression with only subtle changes understood and accepted by everyone simultaneously. Then reality hit.

Some organizations have put "lead" or "acting" Supervisor positions in place. This is a good step as it gives one a chance to test drive the

Role of Supervisor. If you are not yet a Supervisor and have an interest in becoming one, do the work to become a lead or acting Supervisor. Without that time in the saddle, you may be surprised at what the job entails.

The most leveraged and valuable work of a Supervisor is focused on achieving higher levels of performance. Supervisors work primarily on fostering team performance first and then on individual performance. Effective Supervisors do not work mainly on individual performance and hope that the work of high-performing individuals will magically combine to create a great team. This is a flawed assumption. This emphasis means that your first question in every situation is, "How does this impact performance?"

The Supervisor needs to know what a good job looks like but does not need to be the best performer at that job. Your Role has shifted from one who does the front-line work to one who builds a team of people who continually do a better job at the front-line work. Your focus is now on the team and then on the individual.

This shift in focus is unsettling for some. Think of the last time one of your team made a mistake. Your training and experience made you want to jump in and take over so he would not make an error. But that is a mistake. It is challenging to address skills and watch an employee slowly come around, making fewer and smaller mistakes while he learns the new skill when you could have just stepped in and done the work yourself. Perfectly, right?[4]

A Change in the Rules of Engagement

As the Role changes, so do the Rules of Engagement.

As a peer, you could talk anytime, anywhere with anyone and about almost anything. The impact of your conversation over a beer after work

---

[4] I've always wanted a font for sarcasm. If one existed, I would have used it here.

was limited to the influence you had as an individual. But now, at all times and in all circumstances—even when you suggest otherwise—you are a Supervisor. When a former peer sees you in the bean aisle at the grocery store, they see you as their Supervisor. When you are at your child's soccer game, your fellow employee sees you as their Supervisor. At the Christmas party? Supervisor. In the kitchen for a slice of birthday cake? Supervisor. At the dentist's office? You get it: Supervisor. Everything you say (and don't say) is heard first through the filter of your new role: Supervisor. The Rules of Engagement have changed.

Moreover, when, how, coworkers and other leaders interact with your changes. And that change is dramatic. Urgent and Important issues intersect demanding your immediate attention regardless of your to-do list. [5]

Being moody is a luxury you no longer have as a Supervisor.

When you worked as a front-line employee, you could dismiss interruptions for any number of reasons. If someone called with a complaint, you would rightly send him on to a Supervisor. If an outsider touring the organization asked an awkward question, you could refer to the Supervisor. If a coworker complained bitterly about a perceived injustice, you could engage… or not… depending on your mood. But those luxuries are no longer available to you as a Supervisor.

In your Role as Supervisor, you are now the Keeper of the Culture, the performance coach, the quality inspector. Whether you feel like it or not. Busy or not, caffeinated or not, happy or sad, you must engage. And you must engage unselfishly with the larger picture as your guide. As a Supervisor, you are always on.

Pay close attention to those times when you want to just let things

---

[5] The Eisenhower Method comes from a statement he made: "I have two kinds of problems, the urgent and the important. The urgent are not important, and the important are never urgent."

go, to walk past the inappropriate conversation, to overlook shoddy work. When I've done that, it's almost always because I just don't feel like dealing with it right now. In a flash, I convince myself that the timing isn't right, or that there is a more pressing matter on my list, or that I am not the right person to address what I observe. But that is nearly always a mistake. When I'm the most effective, and when Supervisors I've admired over the years are the most effective, it is because of a total engagement mindset. As a Supervisor, the Rules of Engagement have changed.

A Change in Relationships

If you and I were good friends before your promotion, our Relationship would change. Read that sentence again. Slowly.

At the minimum, and only when we are both mature and professional, the topics of conversation at and away from work will change.[6] Usually, however, friendships change and go through a bit of distancing. Then, if performance issues arise, even small ones, the bond is tested. More often than I can recount, well-intentioned people have accepted the promotion to Supervisor and assumed nothing would change between friends. Then, when the supervised friend resists performance management efforts, the friendship fractures.

Consider carefully the change in friendships Supervisory promotions always create. Talk with your friend before accepting the job and clarify expectations. Identify the new Rules of Engagement. Talk openly about how you will handle it when (not *if*, but *when*) conflict arises. Then put a review of expectations on your calendar (three months after starting as

---

6 I've known several supervisors who have managed this change well. But, among the thousands I've met, this number is relatively small. Both parties to the friendship must be exceptionally mature and humble. And they must establish new "Rules of Engagement" in advance. For example, some have agreed that they will never talk about work outside of work. Some have decided they will defer any disciplinary or coaching duties to other members of the supervisory team.

Supervisor) and discuss your expectations as they have played out in real life experience. This, of course, only works with mature friendships and professional people.

A Change in Resources

As a Supervisor, your view of Resources also changes. When you were a peer, you were concerned about your own job and the impact any resource decision had on you personally. Beyond that, while you were interested in the effects these decisions had on your teammates and friends, it was usually just that: **interest**.

The decision to forego investment in football-shaped ergonomic keyboards with fingerprint security was interesting to you only because two of your co-workers complained of wrist problems. You had an opinion, of course, but beyond that, you had little *influence*. Your view of Resources was limited.

But now, from the Supervisor's vantage point, new chairs, complex staffing, personal heaters, training dollars, and broken microwave ovens all impact you.

Many organizations involve Supervisors in building out the annual budget. Some Supervisors even have responsibility for managing segments of the budget.

As a front-line employee, you were concerned about one personal space heater. As a Supervisor, you are now concerned about 30 space heaters, 30 power strips, overload on the building's circuits, maintenance and replacement costs, new wastebaskets, training and reminders about how close the space heater can be to systems, background noise, melting Hershey bars, and naps. You get the idea.

> *Simple decisions about Resources are not so simple in your new role as Supervisor.*

A Change in Responsibilities

As a front-line employee, you were mainly responsible for yourself. If a co-worker didn't show up on time, you were not responsible for saying or doing anything. If she consistently made mistakes, you would never be called to account for her blunders. While you cared about the probationary employee's success, partly because you were tired of overtime (not the money, just the overtime), you were not responsible for her progress.

As a Supervisor, you are responsible for the performance of the team *and* the individual. When a performance problem arises, you are responsible for looking first at the structure in which the problem is demonstrated and change it. Or, at the minimum, lobby to change the structure. Then you are responsible for looking at your contributions to the problem. Are your expectations clear? Are they well communicated? Are they realistic? Have you provided coaching and training? Once you are clear that the structure is appropriate and not contributing to the problem, and once you are assured that your expectations and support of the employee are excellent, then the responsibility of the problem shifts wholly to the employee. But only then.

Point of Leverage

1. Consider the Five Rs that have changed since you became a Supervisor: Role, Rules of engagement, Relationships, Resources, and Responsibilities. Which of the Five Rs are you experiencing the most?
2. Which of the Five Rs is the most significant change you are experiencing?
3. Identify someone who is good at managing this change. Interview her about how she does it.
4. Pick one habit she has and practice it for three weeks.

Resilient Supervisory Skill #4: Whenever a change in Roles occurs, clarify in writing and in conversation the change in the other Rs of the supervisory relationship.

Chapter 5:

Bring your Brain to Work--The Power of Assumptions

Our brain is primarily a survival mechanism. You are reading this, so yours is working. Its drives and mechanisms are fundamentally about survival. Therefore, our brain conserves energy. And it is very good at it.

The survival system is augmented by a habit system. Its purpose is to turn decisions, actions, and complexity into pre-programmed habits, each requiring almost no energy to maintain.

Test it. Get someone's attention and toss him your keys. Without flinching, without conscious complex decision making, and without an act of will, he will merely catch the keys. Habit. If he is a stranger, you may lose your keys, so apply a bit of judgment here. Or not and tell the story later. Your choice.

Above the habit system is our brain's goal system. Its purpose is to focus, decide, plan and execute. It is the system that imagines a different future and acts to get it. It is the slowest and most energy-intensive of our systems. If you are concentrating on these words right now and finishing each sentence before your eyes get to the period, you are using this system. If your mind wandered as you read these words and you now just realized it, you were in your survival system. If you got up, poured a cup of coffee, returned to a comfortable seat, without spilling the coffee while you thought of buying a different car, you were in your habit system. Pretty amazing.

The survival system is the default in our brain. Think of it this way: our brain only does what it needs to do to survive unless prompted (intensely) to shift up into the habit or goal systems.

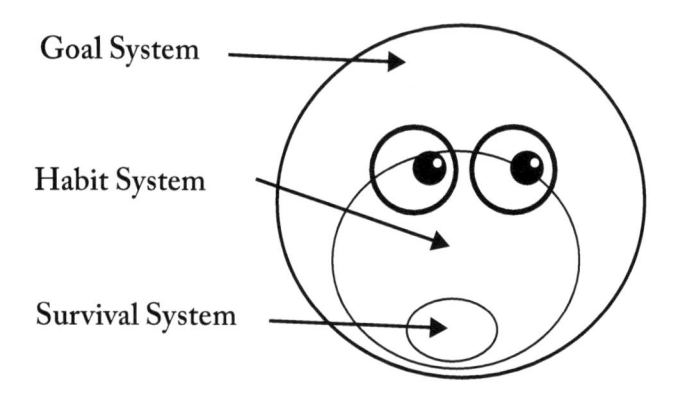

With this understanding, let's think about your mental models. Have you experienced any conflict, any bumps in the road, recently? Good. Those speed bumps, or sharp left-hand turns, are an invitation to see your mental models clearly, to learn and adjust them. Your brain will not naturally look at mental models unless prompted to do so. It takes too much concentration, too much energy.

Imagine that someone ignores your suggestion (or even your directive). This is a prompt to pump the brakes and think about your mental models. It's a mental speed bump. Rather than downshifting and powering over the person, slow down and look at your mental models. You may, like Cartman on *South Park*, want to shout, "You will respect my authoritah!" But slow down for a moment.

What is your authority? Where does it come from? Why do you think that person should "respect" it? Can you be effective even if someone does not respect your authority? Can you be effective without authority?

Speed bumps, from minor inconveniences to outright conflict, give us an opportunity to check our mental models. Don't miss the chance. Take advantage of these interruptions. Your assumptions were built over some time, and they will only be updated through the speed bumps of conflict.

"Just Enough" Focus and Attention

One of the most exciting and efficient mental operations we have is demonstrated by our ability to pay attention to *just enough* of what is going on around us to survive. We do not observe and "record" everything we perceive. Instead, we are usually very good at paying attention to *just enough* data points to connect the dots. We don't see the world as it is. We see it close enough to reality to function.[7] We see the world as we think it is.

> *We do not see the world as it is. We see it as we think it is. And that is usually close enough to function quite well.*

Approaching a crosswalk, we do not see the leaves on the trees or the fourth car, but just the flow of traffic and the first car. We do not know how many people are in the first car, but only the driver. We don't see the license plate, but only the bumper. We don't see the color of the windshield, but just the color of the hood. We don't know the brand of tires. But when we're asked about all those things, we are often quite confident in what we have "seen." This confidence comes from the amazing superpower we have that enables us to fill in the blanks, to sketch in what we have not actually seen, and approximate reality. This is one of the purposes of our reticular activating system. This specific

---

[7] Some have wisely observed that we don't see the world as it is, we see it as *we* are. This is especially true when we are annoyed with people. Often our annoyance reveals much more about us than it does about the goober in front of us. "Quote By Anaïs Nin: "we Don't See The World As It Is".

region of the brain helps us create patterns of observation and thought so that we can turn down the noise of our perceptions and only "see" or "hear" or "feel" what is necessary for minute-by-minute survival. It is also how we organize sophisticated mental models or assumptions about the world in which we live.

We do this by using mental rules to fill in the blanks. A rule of consistency applies: If it's a blue hood, the entire car is blue because vehicles are painted in one color. A rule of gender suggests if a 30-year-old looking woman is driving the car, the children in the back seat are hers. It is mildly unsettling to discover that the blue color on the hood doesn't match the grey of the rest of the car. And that the children in the back seat were not her two elementary-aged daughters on the way to school, but golden retrievers she walks for her part-time job.

These rules by which our mind fills in the blanks are worthy of our attention. I call these rules assumptions. This Power of Assumptions has long fascinated me. I've been keenly aware of the impact flawed assumptions have on leaders, Supervisors and entire organizations. And at the effect, they have on whole professions and cultures.

As a Supervisor, you assume (make a rule, observe some details and fill in the rest) that someone who used to work for State Patrol Dispatch is great at traffic calls but does not know how to deal with domestic violence. You assume that a new hire who worked as a greeter at Walmart is old and is afraid of technology. You believe that a shop steward argued with the rule because she hates management. You presume since the last CAD upgrade was a bear to learn then this next one will be worse. You assume that younger people, who seem to always be on their smartphones, don't know how to have "real" relationships. Perhaps you assume that an electric car uses fewer resources than a gas-powered car because it gets better "mileage." Think again.

To compound the complexity of this dynamic, most people do not know these assumptions exist. Most live as though they experience the world directly and as it is rather than indirectly, and in large part, through filters and lenses that I call assumptions.

BRING YOUR BRAIN TO WORK--THE POWER OF ASSUMPTIONS

Often saying, "No that's not how it is, but that's how you saw it," creates high anxiety and even anger. But we cannot be resilient leaders and Supervisors unless we master this concept: We lead by challenging assumptions.

> *Noticing assumptions that function like mental lenses through which we view ourselves, our work and our co-workers, is a vital skill. Ensuring the accuracy of those lenses is even more crucial.*

How often have you been 100% sure of something only later to discover you were wrong? Or partly wrong. Wrong-*ish*. When we pause to think about it, our world and our work are full of examples we are now convinced of that are fundamentally different than what we used to be sure of. Do you know what causes most stomach ulcers, for example? Do you know what even moderate sleep deprivation does to your blood sugar levels? Do cellphones cause fuel pumps to explode into flame? Do you know why the United States is not a Democracy but a republican form of government?[8]

Look at that grouchy expression on the face of the older man across the room. Whatever you believe to be true of him is probably incomplete at the least and likely utterly incorrect at the most.

Some things, of course, are objectively right, and adjusting our assumptions, and mental models make little difference. Gravity still works. The sun rises in the east. Brussels sprouts are disgusting no matter how they are prepared. Objective truth exists. But most of the constructs we live within, while experienced as objective truth, are models made up of what we assume to be true.

That's not the problem. The challenge lies in the experience of reality those assumptions create. Concentrate with me here, this is important.

---

8   Republican form of government does not refer to the Republican Party but to a construct. Look it up. You may be surprised, but I hope not.

Our mind looks through the assumptions and mental models like the eye gazing through a lens. Sometimes (more often than we care to admit) the lens is distorted.

To complicate matters, we are unaware of the distortion. We settle into a mental model, making assumptions, and then function as though we have discovered the truth. Our partial observations are experienced as in-depth research. Our incomplete experience feels like expertise. Our mind is made up. Then it searches for confirmation. And finds it. It's as though the Jack Russell Terrier in our brain gets a scent and keeps moving until it sees more.

- » That trainee isn't very verbal. He won't make it. Six months pass, and he fails.
- » Janet has only been with the company for two years. She'd never make a good Supervisor.
- » Brett came from South Dakota. He can't make it in a city.
- » Assumption: People know where they are.

If our assumptions—our mental models—are the lenses through which we perceive and then experience the world, it follows that they need to be as accurate as possible. This means that as leaders and Supervisors, our fundamental work is to help our team adjust assumptions and mental models.

Furthermore, the most potent skill resilient Supervisors have is their ability to see their own assumptions and adjust them to more closely fit reality. Practicing that skill on myself makes me better at spotting incomplete assumptions others have and helping them adjust accordingly.

Point of Leverage

This might be the most leveraged of all Points of Leverage.
1. First, think about assumptions you've had about coworkers that, after time, were proven to be incomplete or incorrect. It is especially helpful if you think of ones that were negative at first but later changed to positive.

2. How did you change your assumption?
3. Second, think of a conclusion or assumption you've recently reached about another person at work. Deliberately set out to discover another way of thinking about him or her. Pay attention to what your mind does with that task. Notice that, at first, it will be difficult to think new thoughts, but if you keep at it, your thoughts will suddenly tip, and you will find it easier to see what you hadn't seen before. Again, this is easier to illustrate if your original, loosely held thoughts, were neutral to negative and if you search for more positive observations.
4. Or, even more, fun, as you drive to work tomorrow, notice drivers who are particularly annoying. This will not take long. Notice what you are thinking about them. Then deliberately explain their driving skills differently.

Upgrading Our Mental Models and Assumptions

As a leader, you can help others upgrade their mental models and assumptions. This skill is fundamental to developing resilience. Remember, most of your team is unaware that they have anything closely resembling a lens or an assumption through which they experience themselves and the world. So tread cautiously and with genuine, respectful curiosity.

When you hear an incomplete assumption or a faulty mental model, start asking questions. A word of caution: Check yourself. Watch your tone and intent. If you attack, they will merely reinforce their current assumptions.

Begin by asking, "Why do you think that? What has your experience been?" As your team member explains why she thinks she will never be able to learn the new software, you can hear her assumptions?

Ask, "How long have you believed that?" Then ask, "Could you be missing anything?"

Getting a specific and immediate response is not the purpose of the question. A time-delayed reaction is. In the hours that follow, she will likely begin to wonder if her mental models need an upgrade, especially if you respect her. She will become slightly curious about what she's missed. Especially if her assumption does not arise from fear.

Think Correctly about Work

One of our challenges as leaders and Supervisors lies in helping our teams think correctly about their work. Here's an example: If a front-line employee believes her value arises from achieving expertise in a specific body of knowledge and technology, and then guidelines change that require new skills, she will think her value is threatened by the change. Her mental model is one of static expertise. A "static expertise" assumption is in place if she believes that her specific, unchanging skill set is what creates her value. If, however, she considers her value at work comes from being able to learn and adapt quickly, she then knows her value increases every time she masters a new skill or adjusts to a new change. Her expertise lies not in being good at something, but rather in being *good at getting good* at whatever comes her way. She is what I call a dynamic expert. Notice that the only difference between a static and dynamic expert is in the underlying assumptions. Dynamic experts are resilient. Static experts are not.

    A leader in one of my companies, frustrated with a newly hired employee, remarked that he feels like he employs three people: The person he thinks they are, the person they think they are, and the person they actually are. Exasperated, he drew three unconnected circles in the air describing how far apart they are. "What we want," he said, "is for these three people to mostly overlap!" He illustrated the power of mental models. Ours and theirs.

Grandmother, Counselor, Dispatcher

A very kind, warm, affectionate and thoughtful Supervisor at a 9-1-1 communications center in California proudly thinks of herself as the nurturing grandmother of the teams she supervises. She remembers everyone's birthday, is emotionally tuned in, knows children's and pet's names, and wants everyone to feel loved and supported.

Sounds great, doesn't it? Her mental model, of which she is very proud, keeps her from having crucial conversations when someone is not performing. She energetically defends all behavior to outsiders. Even if those outsiders are other Supervisors or members of the administrative team. Her mental model of what her job is makes her ineffective.

Consider Andrea worked for five years as a crisis line counselor before coming to work as a Call Receiver and Dispatcher in the 9-1-1 Center. She took the job because she thought she could help more people in their most significant moments of need. She applied that mental model to her team members as well, often hitting the "unready" key to continue a conversation about parenting, marriage, stress management or relationships.

When on a call, Andrea's counselor training kicked into full gear. Her call times were 5 to 10 times longer than her peers. Data entries were sparse and often incorrect as she focused on connecting with the callers. Her mental model of herself and her job created a significant conflict with her team and her Supervisor. She is now working as a waitress at a truck stop. And loving it. And making huge money in tips. Go, girl!

Point of Leverage

Think about your work. Ask yourself these three questions:
1. What is this job?
2. What does excellence look like in this job?
3. What assumptions do I need to change to become excellent at this job?

Resilient Supervisory Skill #5: Check your Assumptions.

Chapter 6:

Listen to Mental Models--The Dog Whistle of Leadership

You've heard it before: Whether you believe you can or can't, you're probably right.[9] Of course, sanity and physics set very real boundaries. "I can fly!" Probably not. At least not for long. "I'm the best singer in America! Those judges don't know what they are doing!" Well…

Listen carefully to what your team thinks is true. Listen for the rules they use to explain their work. It is especially helpful to listen when people are complaining. Those moments (while mildly irritating) provide a glimpse into the invisible mental models they use as Rules of Engagement.

When the opportunity presents itself, just ask, "Why do you think that?" (Caution: if you are sarcastic, this will backfire.) Inquire with genuine, respectful curiosity about what the team member thinks and why she thinks it is true. Ask how long she's considered it. Then ask if there might be another plausible way of thinking. Spark curiosity.

---

9   Attributed first to Henry Ford.

If you assume a co-worker doesn't care, then his behaviors bother you. But those same behaviors take on a very different meaning when you believe that he has good intentions and cares just as much as you do. He just focuses on slightly different themes.

Practice this with yourself, especially with emotional assumptions. When you begin to form a snowball of emotional explanations that become an avalanche of stupidity, stop and ask yourself why you think that. Ask yourself how long you've thought it. Be careful. You will feel like making a long list and feel like it's been this way forever. Slow your roll. Ask yourself, genuinely and respectfully, what you are missing. This is difficult but essential. All resilient leaders do this. It does not get much easier with practice, but it also won't get more difficult. The stakes just get higher.

Conflict is an Invitation to Check My Assumptions

Conflict is also an invitation to check assumptions. It is a signal to check what you believe is true. Like the check engine light on the dash of your car, conflict signals that some generic assumption is defective. While it is tempting to jump in and fix the conflict as it presents itself, it is never the right first move. Check your assumptions first. They are the source of nearly all conflict.

Let's Review: Filling in the Blanks Correctly

Our assumptions, also sometimes called mental models, are the tools our brain creates and uses to fill in the blanks between what we directly observe and what we deduce. Our mind works to perceive only enough of the world to make it work for us. We do not need to pay attention, for example, to every word a person says to understand what they mean. We do not need to see every leaf to know it's a tree or see every car to know it's a long traffic jam. We only need to see enough to connect a few dots and create a map of reality. Our mental models, our assumptions, are approximations of reality. They are not reality.

In fact, it is likely that you don't read every word on this page. Your mind skips the words it does not need and feels in the rest to get the meaning.

(Reread that last sentence. Did you see the wrong word? If not, your brain expected to see the word "fills" and changed the word "feels" to "fills" seamlessly using rules to fill in and correct the sentence. Superpower! Pretty amazing stuff.)[10]

Think of the last time someone called on the phone while you were reading or watching television or even driving. As they told you that they were going to be a few minutes late for dinner and went on to describe in detail the reasons why they were going to be late, your mind bounced back-and-forth between oncoming traffic or a picture in a magazine or a television commercial and what the caller was saying.

After the phone call, your brain uses mental models, or assumptions, to complete thoughts and concepts with words you didn't hear. Most of the time the rules we apply to accomplish this feat get us close to the actual conversation.

If someone calls at 5:30 in the evening and suggests he will be late for dinner, describing in detail the cause, and your mind wanders to something else and back, you are probably correct in assuming that traffic on the interstate is the reason.

Occasionally, the assumptions we use to fill in the blanks are incorrect and can get us into a little trouble. This power of assumptions can lead us to believe wrong things. For example, following a presentation to a large audience, I have been quoted as having passionately declared something that I don't believe. I know this is not merely clumsy communication on my part (although, I can scramble an idea along with the best of them), but rather an example of the power of assumptions at work. The listener

---

10 All other typographical errors and errors in grammar were left in, not because of a failure on the part of the copy editors, but as an exercise to sharpen your ability to really see what is in front of you. Or not.

expected me to say something that fits his current mental model. When I did not comply, his brain simply erased what I said and replaced it with something that was more convenient. He replaced my words and thoughts with concepts that fit his preconceived mental image.

When I assume you want to join me for a meeting, and you say, "I will try to make it," I think you are actually saying, "I really want to be there and will try with all my might and God-given talent, giving it Herculean effort, braving weather and physical limitations, to make it well prepared and with a good attitude."

That's not what you said. You probably said, "I will try, but not very hard. And my effort will end the moment I walk away from you." (I'm just sayin'.)

I'm known far and wide for this response to the word TRY: "Oh, ok, so you aren't going to do it, right?"

I don't have many friends.[11]

Our Assumptions Weren't Built in a Day

Our assumptions are built over time. And they are often borrowed from others who, at the time, we regarded (without much thought) as an expert. Our assumptions are usually not very sophisticated. They are based on small experiences that our mind sees as emblematic of reality. If we are annoyed by the driving habits of one Prius driver, we assume that all Prius drivers are similarly annoying.[12]

---

[11] I often compound the discomfort by lapsing into Yoda's voice and saying, "There is no try. Do or do not!" And I'm quite good at his voice. Did you know that Yoda and Grover of Sesame Street sound the same? They are both voices done by the late Frank Oz. Now you know. You are welcome.

[12] Google returns 1.7 million results in 1/3 of a second when asked, "Why are Prius Drivers so bad?" Now that is the Power of Assumptions at work. If Prius drivers are truly that bad, their traffic citations, accidents and insurance rates would all reflect this. You're going to check it out, aren't you?

Invisible Operating Systems of our Assumptions

Once my mental models are in place and serving me well, they become invisible and function in the background of my thinking, much like the operating system on your PC or phone or iPad. They are the Rules of Engagement that allow me to function in a complex world without paying much attention. This is a beautiful thing unless my assumptions are incorrect, incomplete or out of date.

I guarantee that some of what you believe to be valid use as a rule of engagement is wrong. Cellphones do not cause gas station fires. Higher IQ scores do not mean a person is smarter and will, therefore, be more successful. Your state does not have the worst drivers on the planet.

Think about this: Crime is not going up across the United States. It is going down, and it is at the lowest levels in a generation. The dramatic drop in violent crime across the United States is not due solely to better policing. It may have something to do with the removal of lead pipes in homes. (Sounds like crazy talk, doesn't it?)

Younger employees do not learn more quickly than older ones. Venting about a frustrating situation does not make it better; it makes it worse. A Diet Coke does not cancel out a donut (Damn! That's disappointing). Boredom is good for the brain. Multitasking is a myth. I could keep going.

Part way through that list you found yourself questioning my assertions. Even if I could provide incontrovertible evidence supporting one of the assumptions it is likely that, rather than fostering curiosity about the message (crime, Diet Coke, etc.), you pivoted and mentally discounted the messenger.

> *Ahh, the power of assumptions at work. We like our world to match our current mental models and assumptions. When alignment doesn't exist, rather than examining our assumptions, we change the world to fit more nicely into what we already believe.*

On a practical level, we also have old mental models about ourselves. If you believe that it is difficult to learn a new technology or process, it is likely that it will be so. If you think that because something is difficult, it means something is wrong, then you will avoid that exercise at all cost. If you think that change comes easily to some people and harder to others and you are one of the latter, you will likely resist change. If you think that your value in the enterprise flows directly from your expertise in a specific area, you will work to maintain that expertise and resist any changes in the structure or schedule or software that threaten your ability to use that current expertise.

Our Brain's Superpower: Pattern Recognition

Our mental models and our assumptions also serve us in that they enable us to make patterns or categories in our mind. Once we create a category or a pattern in our mind and put something in the category, our brain no longer needs to pay much attention to it.

When I walk into a room and perceive a chair, I don't have to stop and stare at the chair and move it around and touch it and taste it to figure out what it is or what to do with it. In a second my brain can quickly perceive that object, put it in the category of "chair," and then not pay attention to it anymore. The mind also does this with pencils, pastry, peppermint, and, sadly, people. It is our mind's way of simplifying complexity.

Often our mental models about pencils are correct. Perhaps just as often our mental models about people are *incorrect*. Think of the number of times that you first met someone and instantly thought you understood their personality, values, and attitudes. In mere seconds you decided they were "one of them" or "one of us." Only after several experiences to the contrary did you discover that you had put the person in the wrong category and applied the wrong mental models.

I have learned to apply a simple tool to the misuse of my mind's superpower. When I find myself negatively categorizing a situation, a person, a group of people or myself, and notice the beginnings of mental accounting in support of the category, I pause and search for indications of the opposite.

This guy is always such a grouch. He was grouchy yesterday, the day before, and today when I talked to him on the phone. I tell myself to stop and ask, "When was he not grouchy?"

This takes some effort. But I do not let myself believe that what my pattern-recognizing mind now sees is all there is to see. I unleash my mind's superpower on a hunt for when he is not grouchy. And I find it.

She's always late. Lazy! She was lazy and late yesterday and the day before and… STOP. When was she early? When did she stay late? When was she more prepared than others?

While this approach is not as neurologically or psychologically pleasurable as simply galloping away on a quest to find more evidence that she is lazy, or he is grouchy, or the Republicans are evil, or the Democrats are power hungry, or Prius drivers are militant (they are[13]), this approach yields perspective and wisdom. And it has the added benefit of training the mind to be curious.

> *A curious, searching mind makes subtle connections and sees opportunity where others see only problems.*

For most people, however, genuine curiosity is not natural. The mind prefers to see something new, categorize it alongside something old, search for confirmations of what it already suspects or "knows," then settle into long-held, strongly reinforced conclusions. This is like the well-worn recliner of the mind. It would instead sink into comfortable assumptions than put on a coat and go for a hike. That is at least until it has started the hike. Then the mind wants to continue hiking. And categorize this hike along with other hikes. Who knew?

---

13 If you drive a Prius, sell it today. If you are not militant and obnoxious behind the wheel, you will become so very soon. I think it's something in the glue used on the interior upholstery. Get out while you can and avoid becoming one of those people we all talk about.

The Black Hole of Grouchiness

I've had the privilege of working with the United States Navy and Marine Corps over the years as an instructor in applied neuropsychology focused on leadership under pressure. The coursework I lead is made up of seven classes, each one of them containing about 25 to 30 leaders. The classes begin early in the morning. I often walk in, pre-caffeinated, and scan the group. At first, I found myself quickly assessing the personalities of the individuals who were seated in the classroom based on externalities.

Imagine one of the officers sitting towards the back of the room, arms folded, tightly cropped mustache, and scowling at me as I walk in. While the rest of the class talks freely with one another, he sits quietly and watches every move I make. My mental model suggests he is going to be a black hole of grouchiness throughout the class, that he will throw his rank around, and is accustomed to having people say, "Yes sir!" This class, of course, is not that type of experience. I think *He's in for a ride.*

I have lost count of the number of times I have been wrong. Dead wrong. In fact, it has become a bit of a sport for me to notice the categories into which I toss people on a whim. I work to resist this urge for a few minutes while I get to know them during the introductory stage of our coursework.

Without fail—I mean literally without fail—my assumptions about the person, and about the category into which I tossed him, are utterly wrong. I have come to know, and have become friends with, some of the most flexible, fun, intelligent, enjoyable and delightful people on the planet who, upon first observation, I would have put in the wrong categories. My own assumptions, left to harden, would have kept me from knowing these people.

It turns out that he was not grouchy. He just had one of those faces. He became one of my favorite students.

> **Resilient Supervisory Skill #6: Whenever a conflict occurs, identify and correct the assumptions that created it.**

Chapter 7:

Insight from Behavioral Economics

Behavioral Economics principles are fascinating and helpful. As a leader and Supervisor, you may want to acquaint yourself with some of the fundamentals of this intriguing approach. Behavioral Economics is the systematic study of factors that influence the way we make value judgements and decisions.[14] The fathers of Behavioral Economics are Amos Tversky, Daniel Kahneman, and Richard Thaler. Any good introduction to the themes in this science will be worth your time.

One of the most fascinating of these principles is the halo effect. This effect suggests that if I put somebody into a specific category, say a tall person who plays basketball, and therefore assume that they will be good at basketball, I also believe that they will be good as a team member. Or that they will be good with money. Or that they will be good at managing their diet. Or at managing their personal relationships.

---

14 A great introduction to the principles of Behavioral Economics is Dan Ariely's book, *Predictably Irrational: The Hidden Forces that Shape Our Decisions*. I highly recommend this book. The Audible version is also good, as Dan narrates it himself.

But the halo effect, of course, works both ways. It can be a bright and shining halo as the one just described, but it can also be a dark halo. If I think someone is bad at one thing, I might, therefore, believe they are going to be bad at another. This is merely the power of our mental models at work. Remember our survival-system mind likes to do things in the simplest way possible. Therefore, if it is easy to put someone in a category and lump everything else about them into that same category, that is what my mind prefers to do.

This explains why the human mind does not like ambiguity. How can someone be very good at one thing and very bad at something like it? How can an employee care deeply about her job and refuse to learn a new skill? How can I love and loathe my job at the same time? It's just not possible. Or so our survival brain likes to think.

Understanding complexity and ambiguity, however, is a form of thought that takes more energy (read: glucose) than simple categorization. "She's lazy," is much easier to think than, "She's having a bad day." And, to complicate matters further, the more tired we become, the easier it is to think this way.

Resilient leaders and Supervisors watch carefully for this dynamic and guard against it. They do not allow themselves the luxury of a lazy, survival-system-driven mind that leaps to and reinforces assumptions.

The Delicate Art of Changing Precious Mental Models

So how do we invite someone to change their mental models?

If the mind wants to spend as little energy as possible, and if creating new assumptions requires a lot more glucose than gazing out the window and growing one's hair, changing mental models will not come naturally. We will need to create a potent trigger or motivation to facilitate that change.

Curiosity is that powerful trigger. It is the neuropsychological instrument we use to create new assumptions. It always has been.

INSIGHT FROM BEHAVIORAL ECONOMICS

Daniel is one of my favorite people. He is tall, lean, energetic and has a vocabulary to match a professor of literature. After retiring from the United States Air Force, he became a Call Receiver in a 9-1-1 Organization. His energy, love of teaching and deep understanding of what is required to be an effective Call Receiver made him an ideal candidate for a Supervisory position. He adapted quickly, rose to every challenge presented and became one of the most effective Supervisors in the organization.

He loves baseball. Man, does he love baseball! While others in the 9-1-1 Organization use their breaks to nap, read or eat junk food, Daniel perpetually coaxes people outside, regardless of the weather, to play catch. Baseball mitts adorn the call organization.

Baseball also informs Daniel's Supervisory and management style. Every decision he makes somehow references the art of baseball. When a team member has a performance issue, it's an opportunity to coach. When there is a mistake, it's just the first pitch. Or the second. When there is a repetitive problem, it's a strikeout.

Let's pause here in the narrative about Daniel. Did you imagine what Daniel looks like? What his voice sounds like? Did you guess what happens after the third strike? Did you think about playing catch in the cold? If so, that is what I intended.

Your mind wakes up from survival mode most effectively when you are curious. Curiosity is the brain's second superpower. It is how we overcome the inertia of the survival system and the deep ruts of the habit system.

Curiosity is the key to all change.

As an effective Supervisor, learn to develop curiosity for yourself and in those you lead. Ask genuine, respectful questions that unleash curiosity. This is the key to all effective leadership.

Let's apply this idea to the challenge of changing assumptions. **I see three steps that lead to changed assumptions:**

Step One: Notice the mental model. Say it aloud or ask the co-worker to say it aloud. Prompt her by asking what she thinks is correct. As an example, if she remarks, "Our boss just doesn't get how hard our job is!" ask her why she thinks that is true. As she works her way through the frustration, you will hear two things: 1.) Her assumption, or mental model, and 2.) her edits of the assumption. What she says at first will change as you listen and ask clarifying questions.

Speaking our assumptions aloud, especially to a non-argumentative listener, *always* results in edited assumptions. This is an essential step as a leader as well. It is crucial that you edit your own assumptions in the presence of a non-judgmental listener.

Step Two: Ask how long she has had the assumption. This is important. The longer she has had this belief, mental model or assumption, the more likely it will be that she has invested in it. She has spent time, energy, some money and perhaps even her own reputation in it. The longer she has held her beliefs, the costlier (but not necessarily more difficult) they are to adjust. There's just too much to lose by accepting a new assumption. Some people still believe the earth is flat. Seriously.[15]

If an assumption has been held for a relatively short time, we are more open to changing it. If, for example, we believe we cannot learn a new technology, we will likely be able to change that assumption with a small amount of effort. If, on the other hand, we have been afraid of technology our entire life, we will struggle to believe that we can learn this new system. Long-held assumptions have been reinforced hundreds of times as the brain searches for experiences that confirm what it already thinks.

In the case of long-held assumptions, seek to change only the smallest part of the belief. Shrink the assumption to its smallest component and challenge just that. Sometimes that is enough. As an example, if I believe all Supervisors are clueless, lazy and power-hungry, you can help me see

---

15 The Flat Earth Society really exists.

that Jon is not like that without asking me to abandon my mental tattoo of all other Supervisors.

If I believe I am incapable of learning new technology, you can help me see that I can learn one part of one piece of the new tech. Thus, a vast wall of faulty beliefs will begin to erode, and I will create a new category. This is the essence of learning. This is the fundamental job of all leaders.

Step Three: Ask if there is something else to be learned? Ask what is missing? Is it possible that the assumption is incomplete? The question could even be as subtle and simple as, "Could there be something else?"

We don't need an answer right now. The question alone, when asked with genuine, respectful curiosity, creates a small time-release capsule of curiosity in the mind of the listener and thinker. It's like saying, "Guess what?" and then walking away. The listener's curiosity kicks into gear. Curiosity, if it is stripped of stress, fear and judgmental criticism, is a dominant force in the human mind.

Point of Leverage

Try it yourself. When one of your team members says with frustration that she simply cannot learn this new software for this new procedure, ask her how long she's believed that to be true? Ask her if there's ever been a time when she's been able to learn something faster than she thought? Ask her if there's been a time when she's been very frustrated but ended up learning anyway. Ask her if there is another way of learning this? Listen and then just leave her to think. It won't be long before her curious mind begins to break through and breakdown and reshape her own mental models about how difficult it is for her to learn this new thing.

Resilient Supervisory Skill #7: Ask, "What am I missing?"

Chapter 8:

Our Greatest Challenge: Overcoming Our Own Psychology

The most daunting of our challenges as leaders is seeing, understanding, and sometimes overcoming our own psychology. When faced with a supervisory leadership challenge, my friends and colleagues have reported the details to me, but rarely include their own motivations, drives, impulses, strengths, and weaknesses in the narrative. However, resilient Supervisors and leaders are self-aware enough to realize that their own inner psychological scaffolding shapes much of the challenge.

Let's look at some of the fundamentals of supervisory leadership practiced by resilient people.

Fundamental One: Focus-- o This, and You Won't Go Crazy

Whether you are new to supervision or an old hand at it, the fundamentals are essential. When we asked 1,200 people what they expect of their Supervisors, they said three things:

1. Say "Please," please.
2. Say "Thank you."
3. Tell me what a good job looks like and when I've done it.

These three expectations form the backbone of all supervisory interactions. Daily friction will decrease as you remember to practice these three disciplines. Have you done them today?

Perhaps your thoughts flashed to, "I don't need to say please and thank you. It's what they get paid for." If you thought this, you illustrate what I mean by "our own psychology." Overcome your unwillingness to say please, thank you, and point out a good job. It is essential.

Fundamental Two: Stewardship of Time--Surprise! You Will Never Have Enough Time

One of the surprises that confront new Supervisors is the sheer amount of work that must get done. The days of finishing your to-do list are gone. You face a never-ending stream of tasks, projects, and meetings. Oh, the meetings! (But that's for another book.)

Primarily the way to get a lot done is to slow down. Practice concentrating every moment on what is in front of you. Work at the discipline of the Rule of One: Do one thing at a time until it is finished (allowing for interruptions... more on that).

Multitasking, once thought a skill to be admired, is a myth. The human brain cannot multitask. We can only focus on one thing at a time. As the habit systems in our brains are working (we can walk and chew gum simultaneously), and our survival systems are functioning (we jump when we hear a loud sound and grow our hair without mindful, willful thought), we are left with the capacity to consciously focus on only one thing at a time. Some people can switch from one thing to another with great speed (although the quality of their work is suspect when they do so), and it can seem like they are multitasking. But we know they are not. In fact, the more quickly we switch from one focus to another, the wearier we are at the end of the day. And the more irritable we become.

If you have convinced yourself that you can multitask and that you've cracked the code to superhuman performance, perhaps it is just your own psychology leaking through. Maybe you like moving quickly and being busy because it feels like significance. Resilient leaders and Supervisors know that excellence comes through focus and not through rapidly flitting from one thing to another for hours and days at a time.

Fundamental Three: Decision Making and Decision Fatigue

We now know that willpower (the engine that drives our decision making processes) is in limited supply. All conscious decisions (What socks should I wear? What route should I take to work? What do I do first? What do I eat for lunch? Should I apply for the new position?) take roughly the same amount of brain fuel to make. At some point (usually before lunch) we begin to run low on our ability to make new decisions. Each new decision becomes increasingly difficult. Relying on convenience, emotions or momentum, we then start to act on impulse. This phenomenon is called decision fatigue. We just grow tired of making decisions, even small ones. While it is possible for us to decide, the effort to do so is not worth it.

Perhaps you remember coming home after a long day at work and mentally locking up when asked what you want for dinner. Maybe you want to eat better, but after a long day of decision making, you open the freezer and spot Ben and Jerry's Chocolate Therapy ice cream backlit by the 25-watt bulb, clouds of freezing air swirling about. The next thing you know, the entire container is empty on the floor beside your recliner while the theme to *The Simpsons* plays in the background. How did that happen? Decision fatigue.

The keys to managing this dynamic are found in at least these five simple ideas:

- Make critical decisions in the morning
- Group decisions thematically and make similar decisions together
- Make decisions today about tomorrow
- Set up habits so that you do not need to make small daily decisions; food, clothing, schedule choices
- Put decision making back in the hands of the person who is responsible for deciding

Fundamental Four: Worry is Fear on Simmer--What are You Worried About?

I can worry with the best of them. I have been fascinated with the neurological and psychological process of worry. Neurologically, worry triggers similar patterns as those put in motion when we are afraid, albeit at a lower level of intensity. I've come to think of it as "fear on simmer."

Furthermore, worry chews through our decision-making fuel quickly because we come up to a decision, don't make it, then back away and repeat the process. It is as if we "almost" decide hundreds of times throughout a day or two.

A trick I learned years ago has helped immensely. Whenever I notice I'm worrying, I stop, pull out my calendar and "schedule the worry." I reach out a few days, say Friday the 9th from 3:00-3:15, title the entry: Worry About X. Then, when I start to worry about the topic, I simply remind myself, "I've decided to worry about that on Friday at 3:00." Something neuropsychomagical (yes, a new word) happens. I am unaware that a part of my mind begins to work on the problem and by the time I get to the scheduled "worry" time, I've almost solved the problem.

Fundamental Five: Focus on Performance

As I mentioned earlier, the supervisory relationship is a unique one. Of all our solid relationships in life (and the relationship we have with our Supervisor is indeed substantial), this is the only one that has one purpose. The purpose of the supervisory relationship is performance. Specifically, the supervisory relationship exists so that I can do a better job.

The purpose of the supervisory relationship is not to create a working family. It is not to create a perfect workplace populated by friendships. It is not to provide therapy for me whenever I need it. My Supervisor is not an investigator, a therapist or a big brother. The only reason the supervisory relationship exists is so that I can do a better job next week than I did this week. Therefore, anything that has to do with my improved preformance is fair game for attention and focus in the supervisory relationship.

As a Supervisor, performance management and continual improvement is the keel under your ship. It is the foundation of everything you do. Reminding yourself regularly of this makes everything else clearer and less susceptible to the tides of drama at work. It is your job in a nutshell. Nothing else really matters.

Resilient Supervisory Skill #8: When the going gets tough, return to the fundamentals.

Chapter 9:

Connectivity's Dark Side and the Impact on Supervisors

Connectivity has transformed our lives. While I am a huge fan of most of the benefits and consequences of connectivity, not everything this tide has washed ashore in our culture is good. The rise of multiple 24/7 cable news outlets mainly trading in coverage of incident-based and anecdotal extremes has contributed to a growing sense that we are less safe than before and that the impending doom is looming like a sandstorm in the Sahara.

This generalized cultural shift in perception is, of course, contrary to measurable reality. We are safer than ever. Crime is lower. Cars and busses don't randomly crash by the hundreds. Cows don't kick over lanterns with catastrophic results. Buildings don't burst into flame on hot days and consume whole sections of cities. Weather events do not kill more people than ever. But we are more connected, and *reports* are repeated more than ever in human history.

We feel more threatened. The threats seem out of our control.

But there's more. If you have experienced employees at your organization who learned their job before the first surge of iPhones (and subsequent other super smartphones) in 2008-2010, the world in which they came of age was different. They were connected, of course, but without immediacy. They were able to disconnect for long stretches in the day without any adverse consequences. In fact, "disconnected" was the norm, the default of society. They could drive home in silence. News and information were available on-schedule rather than on-demand.

With the advent of connectivity, mostly through smartphones, the change began. If the purpose of all networks is to compress time (read: move faster), the smartphone is the last part of that connected network. It is in our pockets and within reach constantly. Add connectivity to sensationalism and subtract personal responsibility and we get twice as many anxious moments.

More About Networks

As with all connected networks, two things must be in place for them to thrive: 1.) Saturation and 2.) Finalization. Saturation means nearly everyone who can be in the network is in the network. Finalization describes the means by which the network is available to me, at my fingertips.

While landlines reached near Saturation, they did not reach Finalization in that a person would have to stop his car and walk to a phone booth to make a call. Or he would need to put down the rake, walk into the house and make a call. The "last mile" of connectivity took 100X (or more) longer to complete than the first 2,000 miles.

My friend called from Atlanta, GA and connected in 2 seconds. My landline phone rings, I hear it, put down the rake, walk into the house, pick up the phone and answer, "This better be good!" 120 seconds. From hearing the ring to "hello" is the last mile.

Let's get a little more techie: The last mile also refers to the space between the switched trunk in my neighborhood and the specific connection to my kitchen. Imagine a country road with

9 farmhouses each a mile apart. (The farmers would call that a crowded city, by the way.) The phone signal lands in a hub between the nine houses and routes the signal from that hub to my house specifically. That is the last mile if we include my delay between the rake and the answer.

The network was only as effective as its ability to 1.) get a significant amount of people to rely on it (Saturation) and 2.) make it easy to use. Back in the day (it was probably a Monday), if I saw a car drive into a ditch, it was *easier* to pull over and help than to make a call. So that's what I did.

Perhaps we were more community oriented in recent history, not because we were better people with a deeper moral reserve, but because we were lazy. Maybe helping someone out of a ditch was just slightly easier than driving past them to a phone, calling for someone else to help and then living with the guilt and ridicule from those who stopped.

The Bigger Picture

Zoom out. Massive cultural and societal shifts have occurred because of connectivity. More precisely because the connectivity of the last mile has been solved. We are nearly always connected. Connectivity is now the default.

I see a problem, instantly and easily connect with someone else who could solve the problem and go on my scheduled way. It's just easier—and generally accepted—to expect that someone else will deal with the problem. In the minds of many, that someone else is often the government.

I cannot overemphasize how massive this shift has been in its impact on the workforce. Your team members are all swimming in the same cultural sea change.

Make a note of how many times mental models about the underlying locus of responsibility reveal themselves. Connectivity has unintentionally resulted in a shift of personal responsibility. It is easy to blame others when I don't know something. "No one told me" is the hallmark of the connected world. If I could not learn, it was because my teacher was terrible. If I arrived late to work, it was because the Supervisor didn't remind me. If I overslept, it was because Apple's new iOS updates reset the default on the alarm function. These are, of course, all true. They all happened, or didn't happen, and are useful explanations for my actions. But they are excuses.

> *Outsourcing personal responsibility is one outcome of frictionless connectivity.*

This change is not all bad, of course. We benefit from the networks on every level. But the surprising cost, at least at this point in our history, is the phenomena I call outsourcing of personal responsibility.

Effective, resilient Supervisors are keenly aware of this reality and develop skills to remind team members of personal responsibility to balance this new reality. Every significant interaction I have as a Supervisor presents an opportunity to underscore the theme of personal responsibility.

When a team member is frustrated with demands from others, the Supervisor asks her, "What is completely within your control? What are you doing with that control?" When a team member is irritable and rude with coworkers at the end of a long day and complains about how difficult the job is, the Supervisor listens attentively and asks, "What is your part? And what will you do about it?"

Think of the number of times at work when interactions were made more complicated because someone did not take responsibility.

Effective Supervisors are on a mission to underscore personal responsibility. Remind your team members that they are personally accountable for their own behavior and relationships. You will be doing them a favor.

Adjustment Disorders and Other Unintended Consequences of Connectivity

The connected digital age has also created what I have come to call an adjustment disorder.[16] Recall from above that the purpose of all networks since the beginning of civilized societies is to compress time. And our new cultural and economic default is "connected" rather than "disconnected." Since this is true, it follows that we rely on our connected technologies to perform the function of improvements and updates even faster. We expect the multitude of technologies that comprise our networks to adjust, for the better, continually. We expect regular and continual upgrades to occur in front of us and behind the scenes with all our technologies. We also expect to be able to fine-tune every device in our life, from our cars to our refrigerators to our phones to our belts, changing to meet our exact desires.

We can adjust and customize everything from our news feeds to our friendships on social media. Our car seats no longer have four or five positions but an infinite number of variations. The lights in our homes are no longer on or off but can be synced to meet the mood of the person in the room.

I could go on, but the point is easily grasped: everything in our life can be adjusted to meet our most minute desires in pursuit of ultimate, frictionless comfort. In such a world[17], we have unwittingly developed the same expectation of the people around us, the policies and guidelines in our workplace, our wages and the temperature in the room. All of these,

---

16 My description of adjustment disorder is, of course, nothing like the original psychological Adjustment Disorder, which describes a constellation of intense and protracted emotions after a significant negative life stressor from which one has extreme difficulty emerging. Such an Adjustment Disorder makes it very challenging to adjust to the new reality following loss. See the work of Bonnie L. Green, Michael B. First, and Thomas A. Souza for more.

17 Admittedly, this is a description of First World societies. It is also a description of those who have access to these technologies. I am fully aware that many poor among us live on the fringes of this reality. More about that in my upcoming book addressing our relationship with pain.

we have come to believe, can *and should* be instantly adjusted to fit our personal requirements. When that does not occur, we feel something is wrong, or we are not listened to, or we are not valued or merely annoyed. This is what I have come to call the *high-tech adjustment disorder*.

Pay close attention to the early onset of symptoms to determine if you may have developed this disorder.

The first signs of the malady occur in traffic as irritation rises when other drivers do not comply with your desired speed. As the disorder takes hold more deeply, you may notice that every driver irritates you. Then, as you arrive at your destination and your favorite parking spot is occupied, you find yourself leering menacingly at the occupant of the car, attempting to beam hostility through his skull and into his brain stem.

Moderate progression of the disorder is indicated when your irritation rises because the security keypad responds too slowly to your touch or when you nearly trip on a floor mat. And with chairs that squeak and batteries that die while you are using them. A low-level irritation with the world around you becomes more noticeable.

More advanced cases yield obvious anger at uncooperative inanimate objects like walls and doors for being in your way.

The most severe cases of adjustment disorder present themselves in the rise of a critical, judgmental view of everyone with whom you work and live for not doing it the right way. This symptom reveals a sincere belief that you deserve to have it your way because *your* way is the right way. What were relatively minor inconveniences now begin to take on the gravitas of moral outrage.

In my opinion, most grievances filed in unionized environments are symptoms of high-tech adjustment disorders.

Take note of your mild to moderate frustrations. Check your temperature; perhaps you have contracted adjustment disorder.

> *The treatment of the disorder is simple. Disregard discomfort in your decisions. Ask yourself if this will matter in five days, or five weeks, or five years. It won't.*

In advanced cases,[18] the cure will only be realized if the patient deliberately and habitually engages in disciplines that create discomfort in pursuit of a higher goal.

Faster AND Better

The digital age has not only created a connectivity and speed expectation, but also a continuous improvement expectation. As mentioned, every digital device that we own now continually improves itself on its own overnight. In fact, many of our newest digital devices nag us until we let them upgrade and update overnight.

From computers to cars to iPads to phones, every device in our world operates with almost no effort from us. Newer and experienced employees alike bring this expectation into the workplace. We assume everything will be upgraded daily, weekly or monthly. We become frustrated when that does not occur.

Old complex problems are particularly frustrating in a digital age since they do not solve themselves in the background and present solutions, shiny and new when we come back to work. This presents a constellation of challenges for the Supervisor of the modern connected organization.

> *Some things can be adjusted quickly and continually. Others cannot. Nor should they be. Knowing the difference, and communicating compellingly about it, will result in a more resilient team.*

The Often-Misunderstood Impact of Connectivity

---

18 While much of this section was written tongue-in-cheek, the heart of my sarcasm beats with the truth. We are not entitled to comfort. We are not entitled to happiness. The most resilient people know this.

With the advent of hyperconnectivity, almost everything has changed. Those who understand how to adapt their habits, skills, and disciplines to constantly changing connectivity-enhancing technologies will thrive. Those who fail to understand and adapt will fall behind, struggle to keep up, become irrelevant. And they will have no idea why.

Many leaders assumed their position of leadership before the ubiquity of personal connectivity. Specifically, with the advent of the iPhone in 2007, (and other smartphones to follow), a vast economic and cultural shift occurred. Increased awareness of and demand for immediacy by nearly every member of society has dramatically impacted daily life. Increased social/governmental supports have shifted the public's expectations away from personal responsibility and toward governmental responsibility.

The individual is no longer responsible for coping with everything from unexpected weather events to irritated neighbors to undercooked turkey. Connectivity, while it has accelerated learning, economic growth, and advanced the quality of life for most, has also resulted in the vast delegation of personal responsibility to "them."

As a resilient Supervisor, you can ease the impact of this massive shift in culture on your team members by emphasizing personal responsibility. It will not decrease workloads, but it will remove, almost immediately, the time spent on drama in your team.

Outsourcing Responsibility and Making Three Choices

Let's get real. In a connected world, outsourcing responsibility can be a beautiful thing. We don't need to be responsible for understanding the engineering masterpiece that is our refrigerator. We outsource its design, manufacture, and repair to professionals. We outsource risk to insurance companies and headache remedies to Johnson & Johnson. We outsource short-term memory to our iPhones and bills to auto bill pay. This is wonderful. And fast. It is also ubiquitous. Our standard of living has dramatically improved, and so has the macroeconomy because we are able to reliably outsource so much of the responsibility for our lives.

Some of us, however, ride this wave a little too far and end up outsourcing things that we should not.

> *Regardless of how far connectivity advances, it will always be true that we are individually responsible for three perpetual choices:*
> *1.) Whom we trust,*
> *2.) What our perspective is, and*
> *3.) Our specific behavior.*

No one, regardless of their expertise or power, can make these hourly choices for us. Even if we try to outsource these choices, they are still our responsibility.

All effective leaders know this.

Even though a coworker is slow and an incessant talker, I alone choose to gossip. I form the words, pick my audience and frames my perspective, narrating with tantalizing and entertaining detail. No one made me do it.

Recognizing that we can choose the right thing, regardless of how difficult that choice, is one of the most (perhaps THE most) empowering and terrifying realities of life. As an effective leader, it is your mission to help create an environment where teamwork can be accomplished while simultaneously underscoring the real locus of power: individual responsibility.

Practice Responsibility

A common opportunity to practice this skill arises whenever the Supervisor needs to talk with a team member about performance. The Supervisor discusses areas for improvement, and the team member points out how hard it is to see the new icons on his screen.

"What can you do about that?" asks the Supervisor.

"I guess I could get glasses," is the reply.

The Supervisor points out an unusually abrupt and dismissive tone taken with a customer.

"Well, he wasn't listening to me," is the frustrated reply.

"You'll have a lot more of those customers. What will you do to make sure that doesn't happen again?"

The employee is frustrated with his pay and complains loudly about it every two weeks.

"The job hasn't changed in the last six months, and you were happy with your pay for a long time. How have you chosen to change your view of your work? What will you do about it, given your pay will not change in the near future?"

In each of these scenarios, the effective leader highlights personal responsibility.

Not everything we get frustrated about is solved by changing our attitude or perspective. Not every customer becomes easier to manage or every icon easier to see when we change our behavior, but taking control of our actions, perspectives and our trusted relationships dramatically increases our effectiveness. It also lightens the psychological load significantly. It is precisely what resilient leaders do.

Choice is an Amazing Thing

Complex societies require complex organizations. Complex organizations deal with change, challenge, and conflict by creating rules. Rules are part of Structure and take the form of policies, procedures, and guidelines. They are most often put in place with good intention. But sometimes they only solve the symptom and not the root cause of the problem. Then, as with all solutions in complex organizations, the solution creates another problem. Complex organizations are made more complex through this law of unintended consequence.[19]

One of these unintended consequences is the illusion created by ever growing rules that personal responsibility to apply judgement is removed. When responsibility is detached, judgement does not engage. When judgement is not engaged, the rest of the mind is soon to follow.

Highly effective leaders habitually highlight the essential responsibility of each team member to engage and choose. In every situation, the employee is responsible for choosing. Underscoring this reality creates an exceptional, and occasionally exceptionally *uncomfortable*, workplace.

Take every opportunity to remind your team members of these three choices. And remind them that they alone are responsible for making these choices.

In simple situations, like learning a new procedure, the employee is responsible for choosing how he thinks about the new procedure and the need to learn it (this is his perspective). He is responsible for choosing to listen, or not, to the negative coworker complaining that this is just another example of management's desire to make work difficult. Or to listen to the coworker who says that learning is only part of what makes us professional (this is whom he chooses to trust). He is responsible for creating an index card with reminders about the new process and for practicing the new steps during downtime (this is his behavior). He is responsible for voicing his disagreement when complainers get negative (this is his behavior).

We cannot control most of what occurs around us in the workplace, but we are entirely responsible for choosing to exert control over whom we trust, the perspective we choose and our behavior. No one else can

---

19 This Law describes outcomes resulting from attempts to solve a problem. The solution creates a changed environment that spawns a wholly unanticipated condition. The economist Adam Smith referred to this dynamic in part when he wrote of the "invisible hand" of government in macroeconomics. Sending your best team member to a professional conference to sharpen her skills, only to have her return and begin a job search because she is now disillusioned with your Organization's backward ways, is an unintended consequence.

do that. No one made me angry or late. No one gave me a bad attitude. No one put that second glazed, old-fashioned donut into my mouth. No one made me sit and nod passive agreement when Toxic Tammy went on another rant.

As an effective Supervisor, tip your conversations in times of change, challenge, or conflict back to this compelling question: "What are you going to do about this?" When a team member complains about another person, ask them, "What did you do?" Remind your team that they are responsible for choosing. The impact of this discipline will astonish you.

Resilient Supervisory Skill #9: Emphasize personal responsibility.

Chapter 10:

Culture--How It Really Works Around Here

Supervision in High-Impact, high-pressure organizations is one of the most challenging jobs on the planet. You are surrounded by action-craving, highly intelligent, results-oriented people who do not want to waste time and energy. High-Impact organizations attract High-Impact people.

To be a resilient and effective Supervisor, it is vital that you see your job as one that focuses on continually improving individual and team performance. That performance occurs within, and because of, a specific workplace culture.

Let's take some time to wrap our minds around this elusive concept of workplace culture.

Much is written about culture at work. It is often presented as the vague, foggy reason why things are the way they are, a powerful, invisible and barely understood force shaping our actions and values. It's flippantly tossed about as the final argument in a losing debate about change. "Well, that's just how it is around here." The assumptions are often that culture is unchangeable.

Understanding the concept of culture is crucial. Workplace culture is, at its most basic level, a set of individual behaviors reinforced by group approval or disapproval. Groups enforce behaviors, and eventually beliefs and values, by giving or withholding one of our most significant needs: affiliation.

These behaviors are called norms as a way of describing what is normal behavior and what is not. Culture is just "the way things *really* work around here."

If I were to invite you to my house for dinner, we would serve you, take your plate away, exchange pleasantries and wish will you well at the close of the evening.

The second time you joined us for dinner, we would tell you to lose your shoes at the front door, point to the refrigerator and put you to work. You would help set the table, cut the cabbage for coleslaw and help clean up afterwards. We would expect you to hang around for scotch and cigars, ridicule you affectionately if you couldn't stay awake until the wee hours and swap stories of near misses and strange relatives. That is how it really works with my family.

Culture at work is the same. It is the description of how it really works around here. Regardless of how sophisticated and clearly written your policies are, regardless of how your website looks, or the depth of new employee orientation, culture is how it really works.

Most culture is accidental, cobbled together over time. It is a set of normal behaviors put in place to solve a problem or meet a need at the time. Those with the most forceful personalities, or strongest preferences, became the enforcers of those norms. They spoke up when others did not comply. As time marched onward, and even as the impetus of the original behaviors disappeared, the norms remained. They became the standard way of doing things.

This is what I call an "accidental" culture. From eight-hour work schedules to locking file cabinets, from poorly striped parking lots to noisy conference room chairs, from half-hour lunches to half-planned meetings, the workplace is a messy collection of behavioral relics all stacked together to create a culture. Accidental culture is an amalgam of agreements about the way it works around here. Few, if any, of these agreements were put in place with an eye to long-term impacts.

Do You Have Any Spam Cans?

During World War II, many islands in the South Pacific lived on a salty, meat-ish canned product called Spam. It was more nourishing than dirt and needed an acquired taste. It served a noble purpose: keep people alive when fresh food was in short supply.

Today, the need for Spam has disappeared, but it is still a staple in the diet of many Island cultures. People eat it for breakfast with eggs and for dinner with rice. Spam sales globally have not slackened. My business partner, Donnie (a descendant of Guamanian parents) smiles, laughs and eats Spam with delight (and a hint of guilt). He knows it is not good for him. Admittedly I also get a little giddy when he makes a feast including the suspicious salty oddity.

But it's not good for me. No one on the planet thinks Spam is good for them. But we still choose to eat it.

Some cultures have a version of Spam in them as well: norms, habits, behaviors that were adopted in another time and served a purpose but are no longer necessary. Behaviors and habits that slowly erode the health of the organization but that we keep doing because we like them so much. These Spam cans exist in your workplace too.

Perhaps your Spam is allowing a team member to toss her phone aside after a difficult call and loudly berate all customers as a stupid waste of skin. Perhaps venting is your favorite can of Spam. Maybe your team loves spouting frustration so all can hear. Regardless of all common sense and research outlining the destructive impacts (to the individual and the team) resulting from a culture where venting is accepted, you like it. So it continues.

Perhaps your Spam can is the "We have it so hard; this job is so stressful" mantra where individuals think that no one else has it this hard. Perhaps your Spam can is the mindset that Management is only motivated by numbers, so you must have an adversarial labor/management relationship.

All of these and more may have been appropriate at some point. They might have been the best you could muster. But now they are Spam. They remain, not because they are correct and right and powerful, but because you like them.

> *Unhealthy behaviors remain, not because they are correct and right, but because we like them.*

But healthy cultures are not accidental. They are intentional. Norms and habits are regularly inspected, as a matter of course, and intentionally changed to fit current needs. The usual mindset and behaviors of a healthy culture are ones of conscious, thoughtful adaptation. The discipline of seeing, evaluating and changing norms falls to the Supervisor. It is your job to notice, assess and address behaviors that no longer serve the mission.

The Keepers of the Culture

The Supervisor is the Keeper of the Culture. You are the one who both establishes and enforces behavioral norms. If there is anything in your workplace that is unproductive, look first to yourself as the Supervisor. It is your culture. Your behavior and the behavior you allow is the culture. It may seem stark or harsh, but what you permit, you promote.

> *What you permit, you promote.*

As a Supervisor your standard of behavior (your habits, your actions, your attitudes, and disciplines) **are** the culture. While senior management can set the direction of the organization, it is the Supervisor who creates and keeps the culture.

> *While traveling, I often hear the distant airport voice entreating travelers, "If you see something, say something." Timely advice for Keepers of the Culture. If you see something and do not say something, you are saying something. You are saying, "Go ahead. That's fine with me. Keep it up, Snookums. Here's a cookie."*

If culture is how it really works around here, then the challenge and responsibility of every Supervisor is to create an Intentional Culture. One in which every norm is precisely what they should be. Look around for Spam cans and replace them with intentional behaviors and norms.

Norms are Always Twins

Effective norms come in pairs: the norm and the reinforcing norm. If it is a norm to arrive ready to work ten minutes before your scheduled start time, it must pair with another norm that is enacted when you show up thirty seconds before start time. There must be a consequence for violating the first norm. The consequence, however small, is the reinforcing norm.

If the intentional norm of a healthy culture is to ask for a ten-minute break after a particularly frustrating interaction rather than venting for all to hear, then there must be a norm that immediately and directly enforced that addresses the team member who curses and vents anyway. If your house is a shoeless house, someone has to say, "Hey dude, take your boots off! We don't wear shoes in this house, Biff."

When a norm is violated, regardless of how small, everyone pivots in their seat to see what you will do. Ignore it, and you've just promoted a new norm. Address it inconsistently, and you've just injected confusion and favoritism into the mix. Ignore it because you're just too busy, or too tired, or too happy to address it, and you've created the "right mood" norm.

At a heightened moment of frustration, Daniel, a newer Supervisor, asked three team members why he has to repeat himself over and over while Amy, a seasoned Supervisor, only has to ask once. In a flash of uncomfortable candor, James said, "Well, you ask us four or five times before we think you mean it. Amy only asks once, and we know she means business."

Point of Leverage

What norms and behaviors just don't work for you any longer? You may like them, they may feel good, but they just don't work. As a Supervisor, you are responsible for changing those norms. If you leave it to others, it won't happen. It also means that your behavior changes first. You show up 12 minutes early rather than 10. You never vent. You take your boots off. Supervisors are the keepers of the culture.

Identify one norm you want to change. Announce you are going to change it. Describe the new norm and its reinforcing norm (consequence). Then make it happen.

> **Resilient Supervisory Skill #10: If you see something, say something. You are the Keeper of the Culture.**

Chapter 11:

Understanding and Communicating the WHY

As a Supervisor, you are responsible for understanding the *why* behind all decisions and to use your judgement prudently based on that *why*. You are also expected to consistently communicate the rationale behind decisions and the values driving them to those impacted.

When you were a front-line team member, you could choose to call in sick with little responsibility for the effect of such a choice. When you had eye problems (I just can't see coming to work today), you could use a PTO[20] day and be done with it.

Now you are a Supervisor, and it is likely that replacing you for a day or more is much more complicated. Also, when someone calls in sick (or *sick-ish*), you are responsible for managing the impact of such a choice, by delicately pulling the levers of attitude, budget, agreements,

---

20 Many organizations have moved away from designations of sick time, personal time, vacation, and holiday time and toward a pool of Paid Time Off, thus eliminating the need to justify if one is "sick enough" to take time away from work. While contracts and regulations vary state by state, this practice simplifies systems and puts the responsibility of managing time back on the employee, where it should be.

scheduling, minimum staffing levels, overtime (and the accompanying bad-attitude blowback.

Along with these challenges, you are also responsible for managing your own attitude, energy, and perspective.[21] Maintaining mental and emotional consistency is crucial to effectiveness as a Supervisor. If you feel irritable, you can't let it show. If you are tired, you still need to move, engage and decide. If you are bored, you need to stay engaged. If you are angry, you will only be effective if you manage that anger and do not let it control you.

The Purpose of the Supervisory Relationship

The Supervisory relationship is one of the most significant relationships we have. And, of all our meaningful relationships, it is the *only one* that has a singular purpose: performance. It is a powerful relationship if—and only if—it is focused on achieving increasingly better performance from a team of individuals.

Focus on performance. Like a compass swinging to magnetic North, let your focus always return to performance. Ask yourself and others, "How does this impact performance?" And, "How will this help you get better at your job?"

Your most important focus is on achieving high performance. Setting and achieving high-performance standards is your best friend. This focus is the beginning, middle, and end of every conversation.

Avoid the traps of focusing on other things. How well your team likes you is not your focus. Nor is their happiness. Nor is your comfort or convenience. Focus on performance. While these other foci[22] are fine and good, they are often the result of high performance, rather than the precursor to it.

When a team performs well, every challenge they face takes on a different meaning. The most annoying problems look different through

---

21 I'll say it again: this is the most difficult part of your job.

22 I feel complete as a writer now that I've been able to use the plural of focus.

the lens of success. Think of the last time your team performed at a high level. Perhaps it was Ice Storm Saturday, or SnowPocalypse Sunday, the team was world class! They loved it. And you were so proud of them, you didn't want to go home.

Did you notice that they didn't complain about the little things? They weren't focused on Supervisory inconsistency or faulty heaters or rude neighbors. They just did their jobs. And did them well. All of their training kicked into gear. All of their intellect and passion and commitment to the mission revealed itself. It was a thing of beauty.

Effective leaders do not wait for epic events to expect high performance from their teams. They expect it all the time. And that expectation sets the teams free.

A wise coach of a professional team recently said, "Winning fixes everything." He was correct. Winning, in your organization, means achieving high performance, windstorm or not.

The Challenge of Consistency

If you have been a Supervisor for long, you've been criticized for being inconsistent or unfair. If you are part of an organization with multiple Supervisors, you've heard it. Even in environments with the most proscriptive and detailed processes, Supervisory inconsistency is a favorite theme.

It is difficult and discouraging to hear this criticism. You don't get up in the morning and write, "Be capricious and inconsistent" on your to-do list. In fact, you think you are utterly consistent. Your internal scale always reads Fair and Consistent.

Resilient Supervisors have learned to stay humble and curious when criticized for being inconsistent. Granted, this is difficult. You may want to lash out directly. Or at least vent your frustration indirectly. Especially if the criticizer is a worthy candidate for your own spicy observations of his erratic behavior. But those approaches are rarely productive. And, as we have learned, they can actually make the situation worse.

Perhaps you work in a shift environment. Rhonda asks to move her break time up by twenty minutes, and you agree. The next shift, Daniel asks to move his break back by fifteen minutes, and you say it won't work.

Billie moves from one position to another after one hour on the shift without telling anyone, and you notice, but it's not a big deal. Then Karen asks to move to the other side of the floor, and you tell her no.

Three hours into the shift, two employees call in sick for the graveyard shift. The policy stipulates that notification needs to be made no later than two hours into the previous shift. You make a note to talk to one of the team members about the rule but not the other.

As you read these paragraphs, your mind raced to similar experiences you've had as a Supervisor or with your own Supervisor. Perhaps you thought, "Well, we were two people above what we needed, and it was slow when Rhonda asked to move her break earlier. We were one person short and really busy the next day when Daniel asked."

Perhaps Billie has had a difficult time focusing recently, and her move to a slightly more secluded spot would improve her concentration. Meanwhile, Karen has been under a performance improvement plan for sleeping on the job, and you want her closer to you.

One team member has not taken a sick day in six years and at the end of her shift last night told you that she and her husband were going to go to a food truck festival. She succumbed to food poisoning fifteen minutes before she called. You decided not to mention the two-hour rule.

You overheard the second employee say, with a loud laugh, that he was going out partying tonight and might be sick tomorrow. He uses all his sick time as it accrues, one hour at a time, and conveniently does not answer his phone when called to help someone else.

You are busy. You are occasionally distracted and tired. You think quickly. Dozens of decisions like these arise throughout your work week. Each one is made with underlying assumptions and rules. The underlying rules are fair and utterly consistent. But those rules aren't often made clear to others. The difference between Rhonda's situation and Daniel's is crystal clear to you but not to Daniel. They are as different as peaches and pears.

Communicate directly. Notice when you avoid uncomfortable conversations. Clarifying your underlying rules and assumptions is an important, and often tedious, part of your job as a Supervisor.

The *So That* Model

Try explaining your thought process by using the SO THAT model. You decided A so that B. Connect your decisions overtly to the underlying assumptions that you use. Of course, not everyone wants or needs these links between the "what" of your decisions and the "why" behind them. But effective leaders are ready to offer the "why" at a moment's notice. They even ask those impacted by their decisions if they would like to know why.

I need you to come in 20 minutes early **SO THAT** you can support the team.

Please attend the staff meeting in my place **SO THAT** you can accurately represent my idea.

Reach out to the customer by close of business **SO THAT** she can adjust her schedule to fit our delivery time.

Detail and gas up every motorcycle that comes in for service **SO THAT** the customer is delighted with our work.

You get the idea. Connect expectations with the result or value you want to achieve. Use this SO THAT bridge every time you engage a member of the team.

You can also use the SO THAT model in the form of a question. When someone asks to do something, ask them, "So that?"

A team member says, "I want to skip the last three steps in the process this time."

You ask, "So that...?" [23]

Clarify the *Why* Behind the *What*

Exceptional Supervisors work to make their underlying assumptions crystal clear and easily understood. They talk about why they make decisions and tip the responsibility of working within those guidelines back to the front-line mployee. Supervisors with advanced skill sets, and a great deal of patience, often answer questions with a reminder of an underlying principle, and then they put the decision to act back on the team member.

To Daniel's request above, you might say (without frustration or sarcasm), "Do you see how busy we are? Do you see that we are short one person and have three trainees working today? Now that you see that, what is the best thing to do in this situation?"

When Karen asks to move across the room, you ask, "How will that help the other Supervisor and me as you work on your performance improvement plan?" I must emphasize this approach only works if you can remove any frustration or sarcasm from your mind. These emotions are not easily masked. They leak out through our posture, tone, and expression and turn a leadership moment into a fruitless fencing match.

Beyond this, when a problem of any sort is brought to you, lead with the underlying assumption, or "why,"-then ask the employee to create options that fulfill the underlying need.

In a conversation with an effective Supervisor recently, he laughed and said, "My team complains about a lack of consistency, and I always tell them to be careful what they ask for." We need consistency about a

---

23 As I've mentioned before, sarcasm is my native language. I appreciate it in others and have mastered it as a fine art. When I use it, and the listener immediately hears the dog whistle of my intention, I am giddy with joy. It's a sign that the listener is completely in sync with me. However, sarcasm used in relationships with a perceived power differential can be quite counterproductive. So go lightly and never use it when tension about performance is in the air. Just sayin'.

few methods. We need a little flexibility with others. We need a great deal of flexibility around still more. But we need absolute consistency about the underlying "why" of any action or decision.

A way of visually representing this challenge is depicted below. The C category represents those few approaches with which there is absolute consistency. Regardless of the situation or individual, we only do it one way. And everyone knows what that one way is. Effective trainers begin here. Effective organizations are crystal clear about the C category. Lean organizations do not overfill that category.

The B category represents those things that can be done in two or three (not four or five) ways, and everyone knows the two or three options. Everyone knows why option 1 works in this situation and option 3 in another.

The A category represents those things that can be done in several different ways. It is essential that every option works. Everyone may have a different way of doing it, but they all work.

Consistency is achieved on two levels. First, by carefully putting expectations in the correct category. Is it an A, B or C?

Second, consistency is achieved by ensuring that the team of Supervisors is utterly aligned around the categories. Unnecessary frustration (and resulting drama) arises when one Supervisor puts something in category C (only one way to do it), and another puts it in category B (three ways of doing it). Or when one Supervisor puts lunch break schedules in category A ("free for all") and another puts it in category C (it never changes).

Use the shorthand "this is an A, go for it, as long as it works." Or "This is a C, we always do it this way, no exceptions." Ask other Supervisors if this is an A, B or C. Some organizations have even posted a large graphic of this model for all to see so that micro-conflicts can be readily solved and perceived (or real) supervisory inconsistencies can be resolved on the spot.

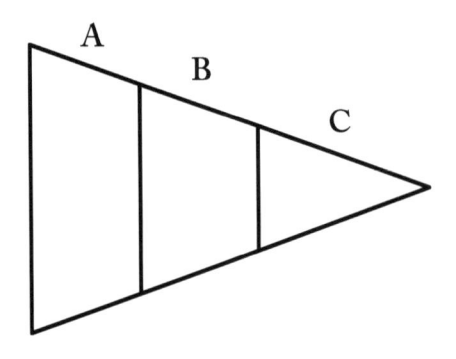

A: Many ways of doing it, but they all work
B: Two or three ways of doing it and everyone knows them
C: There is ONLY ONE WAY of doing it

Point of Leverage

At your next Supervisory Team meeting, list ten common themes or expectations from your work. Then ask each Supervisor to describe where they would put the topic. Is their approach to a specific theme an A, B or C?

Take note of inconsistencies in the team. Debate the appropriate action. Come to an agreement and practice it until the next meeting.

Resilient Supervisory Skill #11: Connect the WHAT with the WHY. Use the SO THAT model.

Chapter 12:

Conflict--The Great Mirror

There are all manner of personality assessments available on the market. Ones that assess your strengths. Ones that assess your weaknesses. Ones that identify how you recharge and how you make decisions. Assessments that help you understand whether you like details or broad descriptions. Some assessments even help you see if you are rooted in the past or want to leap into the unknown future. They are fun, usually instructive, and occasionally insightful.

However, these assessments are all based on your willingness and ability to be just a little introspective. At the most basic level, the assessments only work if you know yourself well enough to forecast what you would do, or remember what you have done, in a variety of situations.

One of the most useful ways of knowing yourself comes through the experience of disappointment. It is a highly accurate assessment provided free of charge by your life. Whenever life says "NO," you get an opportunity to see yourself. In fact, as I told my children when they were younger, the only way to honestly know yourself, or someone else for that matter, is to experience one (or several) of life's disappointments.

I recall asking my children, "Have you said 'No' to your friend yet?" My sons or daughter would recount a time when a friend's response to a "no" was to manipulate or become angry or pout. On the other hand, disappointment sometimes revealed kindness or flexibility or resilience. We can't know ourselves, or others until we get a big, fat "No!" The experience is a mirror and scale simultaneously.

Conflict is one of those times when life says, "No!" It is a common experience and provides a reliable way of seeing our values, strengths, drives, and impulses. It is so useful that we think of it as an accurate assessment tool.

When we look for people to step into leadership in our organizations, we watch for how they manage conflict. Without fail, how they think about and manage conflict provides the keenest insight into internal value structures, disciplines, impulses, and assumptions.

Furthermore, without fail, every resilient Supervisor is a master at managing conflict. They address it when it is behavioral and before it becomes a pattern. They address it with curiosity. They communicate directly. They have learned to not wait until conflict, and the rolling snowball of emotions it calls up takes on a larger and more intense life of its own. They assume good intent. They assume that actions outweigh words by a 10 to 1 margin.

Managing Conflict

But how do effective Supervisors manage conflict? Here's what we have learned by observing them for decades.

First, they take stock of their own emotional response. If they feel angry, they ask themselves what their expectations were and why that was important.

We all know that we have expectations about everything that matters to us. We often fixate on the specifics of our expectations rather than the value that created the expectation. Then when the details are not met, we experience disappointment, irritation and sometimes even anger.

As one of those Supervisors, I take stock of my own emotional response. Perhaps my answer is "stress." Knowing that stress is fear, I ask myself what I am afraid of and why. Then I ask what I am going to do about it. I know that I am in complete control of only three things: whom I rely on, my perspective and my behavior. So I take control of one of those three, take the first step, and the fear/stress fades.

Second, these skilled Supervisors stay behavioral in their focus. When addressing the conflict, both in their thoughts and directly with the individual, they focus on observable behavior rather than the internal architecture of intention or motive.

Rather than saying, "You obviously don't care," they say, "You arrived 30 minutes later than promised." Rather than saying, "You are arrogant," they say, "You are making a decision that is not yours to make."

Imagine standing in line for your morning coffee when the person in front of you backs up and steps on your toe. Staying behavioral means that you would say, "You stepped on my toe," rather than, "You're clearly a self-absorbed fool!"

Third, the resilient Supervisors we've studied are good at clarifying expectations. They know that most of the time, their team operates with invisible and ill-defined expectations. Since expectations arise from values, they know we have expectations about everything that matters to us

If dependability matters to you as my Supervisor and you ask me to "show up on time," you likely think you have communicated your expectations to me, and so do I. We both smile, nod, and move on with our day. Then when I arrive two minutes before my shift, grab a coffee and saunter to my workspace, you are angry. You value dependability, and so do I. In fact, I will show up exactly two minutes before my shift for the rest of my career. However, your expectation of "showing up on time" means showing up twenty minutes early.

Skilled Supervisors clarify expectations in advance of the event. Conflicts will occur at that time rather than during or after the event. And the conflicts will be much smaller, barely noticeable and easier to handle.

They clarify expectations by being as specific as possible and linking the expectation to the value that created it. Again, they use the SO THAT bridge when they speak.

"I expect that you arrive twenty minutes before your shift, according to the clock on your cellphone, *so that* you can get up to speed, receive a briefing from the outgoing team member, settle in, and be ready to go before your shift begins. Arrive early *so that* your team members from the earlier shift do not need to stay a minute longer than they need to."

They often follow up with, "Is that a reasonable expectation?" If it is not, they address it before disappointment and frustration set in.

This approach helps you, and I address conflict when it is small. I call this "micro-conflict." The conflict that arises from missed expectations or unproductive behavior is so small that I can change my behavior, or you can change your expectations in some way, before I've built habits and before you turn into a toxic waste dump of frustration.

Fourth, these skilled and resilient Supervisors communicate directly about impacts. When addressing a behavior, they describe the exact effects it creates. They are careful not to exaggerate or embellish. Doing so will cause them to lose credibility. Drama, while entertaining, does not inspire confidence. "She is an amazing actor" is a compliment on Broadway, not in a team meeting.

In resolving conflict, they think about when the conflict did not exist and discover what has changed. Then they set about RE-solving the conflict. Change in behavior is the only thing that will bring about resolution.

Fifth, skilled Supervisors don't drop the ball. They follow up. All resolutions that last do so because changed behaviors become changed habits. Conscious behavior becomes an unconscious habit through intentional, rewarding repetition. Although habits form much more quickly than most of us like to admit, such formation is more likely to occur if there is a reward in the behavior, if the behavior works in some way. Accountability is that reward. Knowing I succeeded, and that you will ask me about it, is deeply rewarding.

Effective Supervisors put follow-up conversations, specifically about the behavior change that will resolve the conflict, on the calendar. This is a powerful and leveraged catalyst that results in sustained resolution.

"Let's meet in ten days at noon for five minutes to see if it's become a habit."

Leaving any behavior-based conflict resolution open ended, in the hope that change will occur merely from the intensity or force of the conversation, is futile. It is also an open invitation to escalation.

When conflict is repeated, even after it has been addressed directly and a behavioral solution has been agreed to, we step into a fascinating dynamic. If the behavior does not change, we are worse off than before the conflict was addressed.

■ *We do what we do because it works for us.*

One of the most potent axioms I've discovered is: **We do what we do because it works for us.** Regardless of intentions, hopes, and promises, if one returns to a set of behaviors, it is because they work. The corollary is: If one changes behavior and sustains the change, it's because the new behavior works better than the old. Read that last sentence again slowly. Let it sink in. It is a simple truth.

But wait, there's more![24] No conflict will be resolved if it does not include behavior change by both parties. Therefore, "What will you do differently?" is one of the most powerful and leveraged questions we can ask as we resolve conflict. And both parties must change behavior. Assigning blame for the conflict is not helpful as it sets one party free from this dynamic and results in more conflict.

Great Supervisors ask, "What will you do differently as a result of this conversation?" They ask it frequently. Then, when the team member says something behavioral (rather than intentional), they write it down

---

24 To quote the Philosopher Ron Popeil of RonCo of "Set it and forget it!" fame. He coined the phrase even before Steve Jobs' "One more thing…"

and put a follow-up conversation on the calendar. And they follow up.

This is an exceptionally effective discipline. It works both ways as well. End conversations with, "Ok, here's what I will do differently as a result of this conversation." And, "I'll get back to you in 15 days to let you know how it's going." Remember, if it is not on your calendar, it is not in your heart.

> **Resilient Supervisory Skill #12: Remember, we do what we do because it works for us. We change behavior (eventually) if it no longer works for us.**

Chapter 13:

Creating and Leading within a Results-Oriented Work Environment

Every good baseball coach teaches players to keep their eye on the ball. At any given moment a player can be distracted by dozens of sounds, shapes andcolors all vying for his attention. Keeping one's eye on the ball is the most basic of all the fundamentals.

In many organizations, the "ball" we need to keep our eye on can sometimes be challenging to identify. Do we focus on what the leadership wants, on the policies and procedures, on the length of our to-do list, on the clock, or on the noise made by other team members? What do we keep our eye on?

Orientation is the term I use to help answer this question. What are our organization and our team's orientation? What does orientation does it return to as distractions occur?

Effective Supervisors create a Results-Oriented Work Environment.[25]

---

25 Our description of a ROWE differs from others in one significant way: Some call a ROWE a Results ONLY Work Environment, suggesting that regardless of the activity, the ONLY thing that matters is achieving a stated Result (Thompson and Ressler, 2012). Ideally, this is an engaging concept: employees are paid based on results achieved rather than hours worked. However, rare is the organization that can operate this way. Our approach is a Results-Oriented environment in which all we do points to achieving the desired outcome.

A ROWE is one in which the Results individuals and teams are expected to achieve are the paramount focus. Creating such an environment involves these disciplines prompted by the Supervisor:

Discipline 1: Clearly identify the Results to be produced by the individuals and teams and the date by when they will be accomplished. Create a scoreboard with the Results clearly displayed.

Discipline 2: Establish a weekly cadence of accountability[26] wherein everyone reports progress towards the Result.

Discipline 3: Since Results need to arise from a strategic plan, evaluate every new opportunity or change in approach with this one question: How does this help you/us get to the Result?

Discipline 4: Use the Results as the North Star for every meaningful conversation. Weave the Result into every decision and every coaching opportunity.

Discipline 5: Celebrate! When a Result is achieved, celebrate it on the spot in a memorable and fun way.

Contrast the ROWE with other types of teams and organizations. Some are LOWE, Leader-Oriented Work Environments, where everyone's focus is on keeping the leader happy.

Some workplaces are TOWEs where everyone focuses on getting a long list of Tasks complete without seeing how those tasks could be better accomplished. Some are POWEs where the team focuses on unwaveringly following Processes or Policies.

In our experience, Leader-Oriented Work Environments create fear. Task-Oriented Work Environments create busy-ness without a sense of accomplishment. Process- or Policy-Oriented Work Environments create a rigid, joyless bureaucracy devoid of creativity and innovation wherein power slowly aggregates to the keepers of the Policy.

Creating, clarifying and keeping your eye on the Result will simplify your work as a Supervisor and leader. It will be the tool by which you

---

26 Chris McChesney, author of *The Four Disciplines of Execution*, (2014), coined this phrase, and I like it a lot.

constantly and gently steer the passions and habits of everyone on your team. It will serve to deflate the balloon of drama when it floats into the team. It will be the best way to prioritize. A Results-Oriented Work Environment accomplishes both clarity and alignment.

> **Resilient Supervisory Skill #13: Create and Communicate the Results each team and individual should achieve within the next one to three months.**

Chapter 14:

This is Changing. This is Not Changing.

Managing change is one of the most critical supervisory and leadership skill sets. High-Impact organizations are, by definition, in perpetual change. They are High Impact precisely because they adapt quickly and around the right themes.

Look around you. If you are in a High-Impact organization, almost everything you see has changed in the past three to five years. From monitors to middle management, from chairs to Chad's attitude, from software to schedules, from partnerships to critical pathways, it has all changed. And it will change again.

High-Impact organizations are not static. They are not fixed organizations with slow, predictable "model year" changes. They iterate weekly. Every week, if not every day, it feels like you are building a motorcycle while riding it up hill, in the dark, with people tossing parts at you from the roadside, and shouting instructions that change, on your way to a destination that changes, to deliver a package to people who want something different when you arrive. And the motorcycle is on fire. And the road is on fire. And the whole world is on fire. And everyone is tired. You get the idea. (By the way, you LOVE it!)

What is the role of the Supervisor in navigating constant change? Clearly, your part is crucial. Your approach to change sets the stage for success or grinding, disappointing failure. Apart from setting the long-term direction for the change, your part in navigating it is the most important one.

To start with, remember that not everything changes all at once. Though it seems everything is changing when there is a software upgrade, most of the work is not actually changing. It feels like the entire job is changing when schedules change, but most of the fundamental elements of most people's jobs are not changing.

Our research of High-Impact organizations revealed that, over four years, any given three-month span rarely yielded more than five percent actual change in the day-to-day work of nearly every employee. However, when asked, Supervisors of those same High-Impact organizations described the feeling of much more significant change. They estimated that almost half of any given job changed in the previous twelve months.

Getting a new CEO, for example, feels like a massive change for most people. But when we studied actual behavioral or habit changes in the 12 months after the arrival of a new CEO, minimal day-to-day changes for most employees resulted. Changes in policy, schedule, compensation, staffing or structure requiring a change in routines or habits, even in High-Impact and high-change organizations, are fewer in number than it feels like they are.

Granted, occasionally a large change impacts an organization. But these changes are scheduled months, sometimes years, in advance.

So when the "too much change!" chant begins to resound, look at what is changing and compare it with what is *not* changing. Talk regularly about what you see. Doing this will put change in its proper context. It will also alleviate a part of the frustration and anxiety the perception of "too much change" creates.

An excellent way to remind people of this is to use the This-Not-

That approach. Regularly remind members of your team that *this* is changing, but *that* is not. The chairs are changing, but the schedule is not. The physical location is changing, but the mission is not. The packaging is changing, but the product is not. The product is changing, but the problem it is designed to solve is not. The size of the team is changing, but the workload is not. The Supervisory focus on performance is changing but what a good job looks like is not.

Time for a life lesson: When my middle son, Jonathan, discovered that he would change classrooms and teachers between first and second grade, he was distressed. He really liked his first-grade teacher, Miss McGee. He *really* liked her. When I understood his frustration with the change, I stumbled upon the "This-not-That" idea. We talked about what was changing and what was not changing. After a brief time, his young mind grasped the idea and settled into the transition. While Miss McGee remained a bright spot in his heart and does to this day, Jonathan's second-grade teacher, Mrs. Endter, did not disappoint.

We used this way of thinking many times as the years went by. As an adult, Jon loves change and sees it as an adventure.

The "This-not-That" approach is also helpful when a change occurs that is difficult and beyond our control. Even in complex and challenging situations, your role as Supervisor gives you the opportunity to highlight personal responsibility and choice among your team. While the new software is coming online in 60 days, and there is no going back to the old one, the team member does have control over her ability to learn the new system. She has control over the time she spends learning the new interfaces, new menus, and the new workflow. While she has no control over the inevitable bugs and glitches in the software, she has control over how she thinks about this change. Point this out and expect your team to be in complete control of their attitude and their efforts.

Clear and high expectations in times of change are your best friend.

Hard work in times of change not only yields excellent results but also well-deserved pride in accomplishment. Dare your team to lean in during significant change. And dare yourself to do the same.

Point of Leverage

Take a moment today and practice the This-not-That tool. Try it on yourself first. List what is changing and what is not changing. Pay attention to the changes that have a negative emotional impact. Notice that that emotion is usually fear or related to fear. Focus on what is not changing.

Next, apply this tool by identifying one or two investments over which you have complete control. And take control.

After trying this on yourself, use it at work.

> **Resilient Supervisory Skill #14: Begin immediately describing what is changing and what is not changing during times of transition.**

Chapter 15:

The Unintended Consequences of Venting

Venting is a form of emotional rehearsal wherein we reinforce the beliefs behind the venting. While the Venter may feel better for a moment, all he has done is etch the thought more deeply into his mental model, invest his energy and reputation in the theme and make it more difficult to change his mind later. Have you ever vented about someone only to encounter her a few minutes (or hours) later? Did you notice your thoughts? It is like waking up in the middle of a bad dream and finding it difficult to shake the effects. Meeting the person face-to-face triggers rehearsed thoughts, feelings, and frustrations that are barely contained behind a pseudo-civil expression.

The human brain is remarkable on many levels, not the least of which is its ability to perceive, categorize and organize all manner of experiences, imagined and real, into tight groupings. The instant the brain sees an object, for example, it searches for a category into which to place the object. Once the category is identified, the mind labels the perceived object, then prejudges it based on the labels or stereotypes of the category, then acts based on that prejudgment. The action may be simple or complex. Then that action creates a reinforced perception of the object.

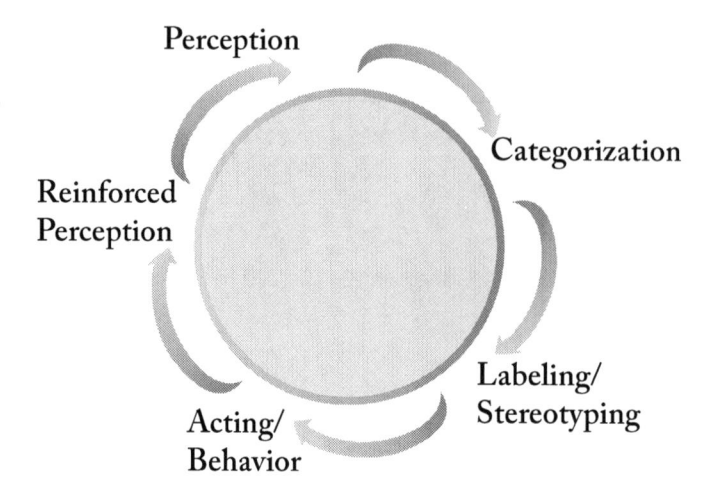

Perception → Categorization → Labeling/Stereotyping → Acting/Behavior → Reinforced Perception

Your brain has done this hundreds of times already today. Perhaps you entered a room, smelled something, categorized it as coffee, stereotyped by thinking, "All coffee made in this specific location is strong and rich," then thought, "The specific cup of coffee Brent offered me will be strong and rich," then you put sugar and cream in the cup before tasting it. This is your brain at work. And it all happened in a flash.

We create categories for everything and instantly put everything we experience into a known category in our mind. Think of the last time you perceived or experienced something that was utterly new and in a category by itself. If you have, it is likely you described it to yourself and others using comparative terms. This is "like" that. The more "like" something an experience or object is, the more our mind will stereotype it. It is neurologically comforting to the human brain to put things into categories. The brain doesn't concern itself at this level with right or wrong but rather with "close enough" and then our grey matter functions quite well. Or, well enough.

I as mentioned above, if you are sitting in a chair as you read this book, it is likely that, at some point, that chair was new to you. You had never sat in it. Because of this fantastic categorizing power of the human brain, you were able to glance at the chair, put it into a category, stereotype about all chairs in that category, prejudge the chair as having

THE UNINTENDED CONSEQUENCES OF VENTING

all the same characteristics of the category, then sit in the chair. The act of sitting in the chair most likely reinforced your category of that kind of chair. And all of this occurred below your conscious awareness. And it happened in a flash.

As a senior in high school, I worked for a time as a waiter in a nice seafood restaurant. The kind of restaurant with soft music, muted colors, warm lighting, white linen table cloths, and vest-clad staff. The customers were generally well-dressed, slightly pretentious, and recreational alcoholics.

I loved the job. Partly because of the team I worked with, partly because of the shockingly high tips and mostly because I learned how to mess with customers. The latter was not supported by management. [27]

On a Friday evening, very near the end of my tenure at the restaurant, a party of ten was seated in my section for a celebration of the achievements of one of the group. The party apparently had begun well before the group was seated and continued through several rounds of drinks. Near the end of the very long evening, the honoree, who had inexplicably named me Butch, asked if I would kindly bring him a cup of coffee. I agreed and returned with a cup. No coffee, just a cup on a saucer.

Approaching the table slowly and gaining his attention I said, "Be careful, this is really hot," and pretended to trip and pour the empty cup in his lap.

He screamed in pain, cursed, jumped up from the table, snatched a napkin and furiously wiped the invisible coffee from his pseudo-scalded lap. For at least 10 seconds.

The restaurant went silent. Screaming Stan stared at his lap, then at me, then at the table, then at the empty cup in my hand. A moment

---

[27] Since that early job, I learned to put people into "mess-withable" and "not-mess-withable" categories. The former is much more fun. If someone I meet has a ready sense of humor, is full of curiosity rather than himself, and a face wrinkled from years of laughter, they are mess-withable.

later, the table realized the extent of the prank and exploded in laugher.

With the assistance of copious amounts of Scotch, we can peer into Stan's slowed brain and see the process. Perception of an approaching waiter bringing a cup. Cups hold coffee. Coffee is hot. This coffee is in my lap. Hot coffee burns. I am being scalded. Anticipation of pain. Muscles recoil. Chair tips over. Wipe the invisible coffee. The waiter is an idiot! In a flash.

This is precisely how our mind works. It perceives and processes everything in this manner. It does it all the time. It is a beautiful thing!

However, one of the unintended consequences of this amazing mental power arises when we misperceive and miscategorize. When we add emotion to the misperception and faulty categorization, our brain can reinforce the falsehood.

Conspiracy thinking is an example of this process. Once someone thinks Vice President Cheney is a Mastermind on the level of Dr. Eviil, their mind searches and finds evidence that fits the category. In a short while, voila! Conspiracy. We have the fabulous ability to ignore contradicting perceptions that do not fit our current categories. We can play a tune long enough in our mind that it becomes our reality.

- *Venting is a rehearsal of the worst kind.*

Listen to Victor the Venter. This is precisely what he is doing. He thinks he's been injured or is about to be hurt (or merely inconvenienced) in some way. His brain searches for other inputs that confirm he is going to be offended and finds them. Venting is a form of communication that accelerates this process. It is a rehearsal of the worst kind.

It is also unsatisfying to sit back and listen to the Venter. The human brain, moreover, is acutely tuned to notice threats and perceived threats. We listen for threats and lock onto them with intense focus. When listening to Venters, our brain tips into fear mode and our body releases a few neurotransmitters that prepare us to fight, flee or freeze.

When we pay attention to an impassioned vent, we join, even if only slightly, in the drama as though it has happened (or will happen) to us. Cortisol courses through our veins as if *we* were the ones attacked or offended. Our 400,000 mirror neurons set up a cascade of mental and physical activity resulting in our own imagined and personalized slight. Venting hurts the listener.

Most of us are not rude. Cutting a Venter off mid-sentence seems uncivil. We don't want to unnecessarily offend, so we listen. Even as the Venter rewinds and replays the Vent, this time with more intensity and added detail, we find it difficult to put a hand up and redirect. And it is likely that the Venter has selected us precisely because we indulge his habit by listening.

Try this: As soon as you figure out that Victor is Venting, interrupt by saying, "May I interrupt?" Then ask, "Have you spoken directly to her about this?" And, "Ok, is this about you or someone else?" Follow up with, "What are you going to do about it?"

If the response is frustration followed by a rewind and replay reaction, interrupt again by saying, "This is only helpful if *you are going to do something about it*. Otherwise, it's not good for you or for me." Keep challenging Victor the Venter with his responsibility by asking what he is going to do about it. Close the conversation with the question, "When will you do it?"

While this is a bit awkward at first, it will yield better results than passively listening and nodding during the diatribe.

Venting is utterly destructive. It is a relic of the past. It is never healthy. Never productive. Go to the source of your frustration. Address it directly. This takes a little courage but is always a better approach than venting.[28]

---

28 By the way, the party gave me the largest tip I had ever received amounting to nearly 50% of the total bill. I was stunned. I don't know if Stan contributed. He didn't speak to me the rest of the evening, and I never saw him again. My manager forcefully suggested that I behave in a more professional manner. I have not taken his advice. In fact, I have a long list of "advice not taken" and of the resulting delightful outcomes, most of which have enriched me immeasurably, that I will share when I'm much older.

Resilient Supervisory Skill #15: Assign this chapter as a reading assignment for your team. Create a No-Venting discipline and make it effective on a specific date.

Chapter 16:

Creating a One Call, One Click, One Conversation Culture

The Supervisor's goal is to ensure that effective communication can occur. Every Supervisor aims to make sure that everyone can know everything they need to know when then need to know it so that they can do a better job.

I am not implying that you are responsible for all communication, feeding passive hungry birds with everything they need. You are, however, responsible for making sure that the team can *find out* everything they need to with one call, one click or one conversation.

> *Your challenge is to create a "One Call, One Click, One Conversation" culture.*

This means that as a team member, I should be able to find out everything I need to know about how to do my work and how to do a better job with one call, one click or one conversation. It is up to the front-line employee to make the call, click the link, and start the conversation. It is up to the Supervisor to make sure that the information is available, current and accurate.

That paragraph warrants rereading.

How close to this standard is your organization?

Most people are curious creatures. And most of the time, we hire the ones who have quick minds and demonstrate inquisitiveness. It is only natural that people want to know what the heck is going on at every level and all the time. Effective Supervisors make that possible. If you do this well, the drama train, which runs on the momentum of half-truth and rumor, will rarely depart the station because it will have no fuel.

"I heard they are making us go to that stupid sensitivity training on Tuesday!"

One click.

"That's not true. It says right here that the training is about communicating under pressure and that it's voluntary."

Mic drop.

"John is retiring, and Randy is taking his place as the new swing shift Supervisor."

One call. Speaker phone.

"Nope," John's deep voice booms. "I'm not retiring for six years, and Randy is not taking my place or even applying for the next Supervisory position."

Mic drop.

> *Build a culture where individuals are expected, as a minimum requirement of their employment, to know what is going on. Never allow a team member to use the excuse "No one told me!" Hold people accountable for using the resources at their disposal and for knowing the facts.*

Establish an "everyone can know everything" norm and reinforce it. Never engage in debate, rumor or drama with a person who has not met the minimum requirement of going to the source. You will sleep better. And so will everyone else.

I'm struck by how busy Supervisors are. I'm also stunned by how much time is wasted on drama, hearsay, reflexive and uninformed decision making, and needless, factless theatre. Save yourself! Clear away literally hours of wasted effort each month by ensuring the One Click, One Call, One Conversation culture thrives and by holding everyone accountable to use it before they speak up.

Tune your ear to dramatic statements that are uninformed by context. Challenge the actors to learn what they are talking about and to come back to the theme when they have done so.

Three Types of Communication

Communication occurs in three ways: 1.) Intentionally, 2.) Incidentally and 3.) Accidentally. Intentional communication occurs in meetings, through phone calls, with memos and emails. We decide in advance to communicate about a specific subject. Incidental communication occurs surrounding an event, often unplanned. The event triggers inadvertent interactions. Accidental communication usually results from something overheard in a casual context. It's the "Oh, by the way..." kind of communication. *In times of significant change, accidental communication is trusted the most.*

Effective and resilient Supervisors are aware of and use all three types of communication. They plan what needs to be communicated in advance and with whom. They are responsive to changes and stick around long enough to communicate. And they are physically present most of the time. It is almost impossible to be an effective supervisory leader from a distance. Management can work by remote control, as it is mostly about direction and supporting systems, but Supervisors must lead up close and in person. There is no other way.

There is a direct correlation between supervisory effectiveness and time with the team. Examine your time carefully and work at being present. You will be surprised at how much more effective you will be.

> **Resilient Supervisory Skill #16:** Teach your team members to take personal responsibility for communication. Take note of communication problems that occur because the information was too difficult to discover and fix those scenarios one by one.

Chapter 17:

Performance Standards are the Resilient Supervisor's Best Friend

Clear, high, measurable and easily understood performance standards are your best friend. Standards differ from Goals. Standards are entirely within our control. Goals are mostly within our control. When your team knows the standards they are to achieve, and when they have effective training in support of those standards, your work as a Supervisor is much less complicated. In the absence of such standards, inconsistency reigns and strong personalities are in charge. Have you been there? I have. It's no fun.

Standards must be linked to the rationale that created them. The "why" behind the standard must be tattooed on the brain of every team member. Effective Supervisors link expected behaviors to standards dozens of times a week.

Example: Reread your emails 100% of the time before sending *so that* you communicate accurately and professionally.

Remember, "So that" is the bridge between what I am doing and why I do it; it links what I expect with why I expect it. Use "so that" whenever you ask someone to complete a task or project. Use it whenever you correct or give feedback. Use it whenever you celebrate excellence. Use it as a question when someone asks you a question.

As an example, Joey asks if he can move his lunch back an hour. Respond with "so that?" [29]

Whenever conflict arises, check to see if you have clear standards that inform the conflict. If not, create them, test them and implement away! Then, if clear standards exist, use them as the arbiter of the conflict making sure to reiterate the "so that" drives the standard.

Ten Characteristics of Clear Performance Standards

Clear performance standards are easy to understand. Ensure that everyone, during and after orientation and early training, knows precisely what the standard is and how to achieve it. Standards contain concise terminology and leave no question as to their essence.

Clear performance standards are directly related to the values of the organization. It is easy to see how this standard of performance helps us express one of our organization's core values.

Clear performance standards relate directly to the mission. The organization's mission should be a realistic, concise and focused statement of the purpose of all our work. It should be able to be accomplished. It differs from a lofty vision statement in that we should be able to say we are achieving it daily. The performance standards are the leading measurements of the work.

Clear performance standards must be supported by tools and technology. When they are not, it is incredibly frustrating. The standard is unrealistic if unsupported by tools and technology.

Clear performance standards are measurable. The measurement must be consistent and easily completed. It must occur regularly and as close to the point of the performance as possible. Measurements that report performance from last year, last month or last week are much less

---

[29] Avoid sarcasm. As much as I adore it, coming from a Supervisor, it rarely ends well.

helpful than those that report my performance in real time.

Clear performance standards measurements must inspire confidence. The measurements themselves must be reliable and meaningful. I need to trust that the numbers are accurate and that they measure the right things. This inspires confidence. Think carefully about how you measure success. Team members love keeping score but loathe doing so about things that don't matter or in an unreliable way.

Clear performance standards are attainable. Most team members are able to attain the standards all the time. Carefully reserve 100% standards for those themes where absolute achievement is essential. Set 90% standards, or year-over-year improvement standards, for the rest.

Clear performance standards are trainable. Our training approach can replicate the skill in anyone we hire, regardless of aptitude, personality or haircut. Never hold the team to a standard that is not supported by training. Expecting the team to learn it on their own means it is a performance *goal* rather than a standard. If standards are not being met, look first to training. It is likely your solution will be found there.

Performance standards must be correlated to the consistency model. As you develop and use clear performance standards, make sure the supervisory team agrees on their placement in the consistency model. Inconsistency about performance standards is incredibly frustrating, especially to high performers.

Finally, clear performance standards are not in conflict with one another. If achieving one performance standard makes it impossible to achieve another, neither will work. If achieving excellent customer service 100% of the time means the team member must give out helpful information, but another standard says she should move people off the phone in 60 seconds or less, neither standard will be valid. Look carefully for conflicts between performance standards and resolve them.

Once you have clear and meaningful performance standards, your entire work as a supervisory leader gets easier. All challenges are met in the context of these standards.

Resilient Supervisory Skill #17: Write out three performance standards that apply to the entire team and three performance standards that apply to each individual. Communicate the standards verbally and in writing at your next team meeting. See what happens.

Chapter 18:

Performance Management Tools

Managing performance expectations is the daily work of all resilient Supervisors. Achieving high performance as a team and as an individual is the reward of the work. A job well done is profoundly rewarding. It is why we work.

We have found that resilient Supervisors understand the central focus of their role and most of them use versions of the following Performance Management Tools.

Performance Management Tool 1: The Power of Expectations

We recently surveyed 1,200 white-collar, blue-collar and no-collar[30] Supervisors in public, private and not-for-profit agencies to discover how effective they were at setting expectations. We asked Supervisors with at least three years' experience to rate on a 1 to 100 scale their ability to communicate expectations with those they supervised. We asked, "How clear are your expectations to the people you supervise?"

---

30 No-collar workers refers to those working primarily in the I.T. sectors.

Their answers were in the 72 to 92 range, yielding an average score of 85 in effectiveness. This meant that most of them believed they were very effective, significantly above the middle, in their ability to communicate clear expectations.[31]

Intrigued, we went further and asked the same Supervisors to supply the names of four people who they supervise so that we could ask the very same question in the same way about the clarity of expectations.

It is possible that you are thinking, as we thought, that the Supervisors might stack the deck and give us the names of people they thought clearly understood expectations. We did not remove this bias. (Imagine me, sitting in a high-backed executive chair, stroking a white cat. *Are those frickin' lasers, Scotty?*)[32]

The 4,800 folks who responded to the survey about the clarity of their Supervisors expectations had a similar response. Almost all of them suggested that their Supervisor was in the range of 82 out of 100. This was good news.

We did not stop there. We asked Supervisors to specify, in writing, their expectations. And we asked the 4,800 respondents to define in writing the expectations they believed came from their Supervisors and submit them without verifying accuracy.

Using contextual analysis methodology that compared the content and the meaning behind written statements, we discovered, even with a very relaxed and liberal interpretation, that there was just over an 11% overlap in responses of Supervisors compared to responses from the top four people they recommended to us. This is to say that while the employees and Supervisors were together convinced that the Supervisors

---

31 I've long been intrigued by the "above average" rating EVERYONE gives themselves. I'm an above-average driver, friend, spouse, parent, musician, butcher, baker, candle stick maker. This is, of course, mathematically impossible. In recent studies, only about 5% of people in any arena described themselves as well below average while 85% described themselves as well above average. The other 10% saw themselves as phenomenal. Apparently, most people are well below average in math skills.

32 With respect to Dr. Eviiil.

expectations were clear when we inspected them, we discovered that was not the case.

Imagine the impact, as a Supervisor, of blissfully galloping through your week believing that the people you supervise know *precisely* what you expect, that they are bringing their best effort to the tasks at hand and working to achieve what you anticipate. Furthermore, imagine that the employees have the same perspective. They come to work believing what they are doing is *exactly* what you expect as their Supervisor. But only one out of ten times is this true. Think of the implications.

If something close to this describes your workplace, it would explain a lot.

Nod and Smile

I have long suspected that Supervisors were attempting to be clear in their expectations and employees were trying to understand. That both parties were nodding, smiling and getting about the work, with neither of them truly understanding what the expectations were. This is especially true when an expectation is translated from a theoretical concept to behavior.

To be specific: Imagine you need to have me show up on time and act professionally. I smile and nod and agree entirely. I'm always professional. I show up one minute before my shift and complain about how stupid the last shift was. I am "on time," and I think my complaining is a sign that I pay attention to detail. It is an indication that I want to do a good job and that I want everything to work well.

As my Supervisor, you think I am chaotic and unprofessional and do not know how to manage my time. You and I both agree that quality is important. But we do not clarify what we mean, so the idea stays theoretical. We both laud the idea of *teamwork*, but neither of us can describe it behaviorally.

Clarifying expectations behaviorally is one of the most powerful things you can do as a Supervisor. What does the expectation look like? Specifically.

Written Expectations

Write your expectations. This will help you make sense of them. Share them with someone who does not do the job and edit for clarity. Then distribute them. Don't do a drive-by shouting. Stop and talk about them. If someone has no comment or question, they didn't read them.

Recently I led a conversation with 50 Supervisors of one of our favorite businesses. It is a chain of restaurants that has been wildly successful for years, and I count it a privilege to work with so many amazing people. I asked them to break into small groups and identify the behaviors they expected of each other that resulted in connecting with customers. Their answers were, in part:

> Have a good attitude
> Care
> Be on time
> Deliver good service
> Be nice
> Be mission focused
> Do a good job

I suggested that none of these were behavioral and asked them to try again. They refined the list as follows:

> Have a happy attitude
> Care a lot
> Be early
> Deliver excellent service
> Be really nice even if you don't feel like it
> Do a great job

Round three: I suggested that, while delightful to hear, none of these were behavioral. So, we zoomed in on attitude. I asked the group to consider what a Server does that makes the Supervisor think she has a good attitude. And finally, we got somewhere.

She smiles, makes eye contact, asks questions, tells people when she thinks they have made a good selection and thanks them. She checks back with the table after five or six minutes and tells the customers how far along their order is and what to expect next.

These are behaviors.

On the face of it, "providing good customer service" seems simple enough. But if you ask three people what good customer service looks like, you may get six different and conflicting answers. If you have been frustrated with someone and roll your eyes and sigh when you walk away, it is likely you felt you were providing as good customer service *as possible*. It is also likely that someone overheard the conversation, saw your expression and thought the opposite. And both of you believe that "good customer service" is essential.

Recall a previous chapter. It is essential to attach the expectation to the value that created it. If I'm expecting you to show up "on time," I should be able to translate that into something specific like, "Show up 15 minutes before the shift begins so that (fill in the value blank)." This clearly communicates *why* showing up 15 minutes early is essential.

It may sound (or read) something like this: I expect that you show up at least 15 minutes before your shift begins *so that* you are able to be completely ready, get to work and replace the person before you as their shift ends. I expect that you will have enough time to orient yourself to the previous shift's activity, read through any changes that might have happened since your last shift, and then be fully engaged at the time the shift begins so that your team members can leave on time.

Another example: My expectation is, even after a very frustrating interaction, that you do not vent openly to team members about your frustrations *so that* you do not make it more difficult for those around you who may have also had several irritating events in a row. Venting makes it more difficult for your team. Don't do it.

Also: I expect that you begin and end every shift, without fail, by reading through your work-related email *so that* you do not miss any significant changes that occur, thereby creating more work for yourself and others on your team.

Here's another one: I expect that when downtime occurs, you practice using the new software *so that* you become as proficient as possible, as quickly as possible.

Notice that those examples are all behavioral. We are not asking those with whom we work to have any sort of internal emotional change to be able to meet our expectations (that is, we don't expect them to become more enthusiastic, or to feel happier, etc.). We are only asking for specific behaviors that result in excellence.

The internal motivations and psychological architecture of the individual's life are beyond our reach. Frankly, even if they were within our reach, we wouldn't want to mess with them. As fascinating as it is to fathom a person's drives, impulses, and their deep psychological motivations, it is not the point of our work. It is not the job of the resilient Supervisor to become Dr. Phil for your team. For example, all we really want is for a person to *sound like* they are respectful on the phone. We are not asking our team to deeply, genuinely and passionately respect thousands of perfect strangers. We are not asking for a person to change their entire internal psychological makeup. We only expect them to act like it. This is a liberating concept.

Of course, if our internal motivations, values, preferences align more closely with the goals and values that created the expectations, and those of the organization, all the better! That makes doing the work (meeting the expectations) easier over the long term. I can act like I respect people all day long, but I'll be tired at the end of the shift. If I genuinely respect people, acting the part is more natural. If I genuinely care that my team members get the rest they deserve, it is easier to show up early enough to make sure they leave on time.

Resilient Supervisory Skill #18: Practice the Power of Expectations

Performance Management Tool 2: Breaking the Bermuda Triangle of Communication

Triangulation is a behavior that creates the most significant damage in organizations. I am triangulating if I have a problem with another person and choose not to communicate that hindrance directly, venting instead to a third party. *It is the single most destructive behavior in any workplace.*

> *Triangulation is the single most destructive behavior in any workplace.*

It is destructive because I must lie to myself and then to the person with whom I am triangulating. I deceive myself into thinking that I've done something productive and worthwhile to solve the problem already. And that by triangulating, I am merely taking the next step. But all I've done is make myself feel momentary control. And I put the listener in a lousy position. She wants to be helpful but cannot.

Eventually, the person about whom I have been speaking will discover that she has been the target of my gossip and trust is eroded. This activity deceives, anesthetizes and corrodes.

Once the triangle has been formed, it is tough to reverse the effects of half-truths, fantasy, suspicion, and mistrust. Some Organizations have allowed triangulation to become a habit and have paid the price of a toxic workplace with increased turnover, buried creativity, and passive-aggressive communication. Many unresolved (and now unresolvable) conflicts began with the triangulation road show.

To complicate matters, my brain naturally multiplies the negative impact of triangulation. If I am frustrated with Beth, it is likely my frustration has been going on for more than a couple of minutes. It is also likely that my mind has begun to search for other examples of this frustration and build a case to take to the perfect, willing listener.

I choose my audience carefully. I would never go to Beth's best friend to complain about her, rather I will go to somebody who is either neutral or, better yet, leans toward my perspective. Then when I discuss my frustration about Bumbling Beth, I edit the story, sometimes only slightly, unconsciously, so that I look a little better, and she seems a little worse. I have spun the story to make me look like the victim, and Beth looks like the smiling, insipid villain she is. It is all very subtle, especially in otherwise well-intentioned people. And it is so very destructive.

While presenting my case about Beth's infractions, I achieve a sense of power and heightened self-righteousness. And I acquire a greater sense of justification. If I continue the narrative and speak to another person, and another, that sense of power and justice grows.

> *With each triangle I create, I burn my own mental bridges behind me. Resolution becomes less likely. Curiosity dies. My mind closes on the storyline of Beth the Bumbler. Correct understanding is buried under sediment of my own faulty mental models and selfishness.*

In my defense, I do not think I am triangulating. Perhaps, aside from a hushed initial whisper from my inner narrator about the inappropriateness of my behavior, I think I am getting advice. Or I'm just venting. And in so doing, I hope the problem will (magically) disappear. I'm seeking perspective, guidance, wisdom, and understanding.[33]

These are the lies I tell myself. But what I am actually doing is trying to feel better, more powerful, justified, more in control and significant. Perhaps even a little superior. Most of the time, I do not see that I am doing anything wrong and I most certainly do not see the cascading effect my behavior creates. I tell myself I'm not triangulating... in this case.

---

33 As you read that sentence, imagine I'm putting air quotes around perspective, guidance, wisdom and understanding. That's what I would be doing if I were speaking this section.

How do we, as resilient supervisory leaders, battle this hydra? How do we keep from joining in the tempting behavior? Sometimes it seems that directly addressing one Triangle merely gives rise to more.

First, it is folly to expect cooperation from the Triangulater. Remember he thinks he is getting advice or perspective. He does not think he is in the wrong, or at least not as wrong as the person about whom he is gossiping. So if the Triangulater does not see what he is doing, and does not recognize the impacts, he will not stop the behavior. There is little leverage with him.

Also, Bumbling Beth doesn't know she is driving him crazy. She's not going to stop a practiced habit without direct communication, and that is not happening any time soon. That leaves the listener. The power to break the triangle lies in the First Listener.

If I come to you to talk about another person, you are the First Listener. It's up to you to save the world! As soon as it becomes apparent that I am talking about Beth, interrupt me. Ask, "Have you spoken to Beth about this?" Interrupt and ask that question before I finish my story.

Then, regardless of my reply, direct me back to Beth: "You need to talk to Beth." If we are part of a team, ask me when I plan on talking to Beth. Hold me accountable for addressing her directly.

This is important. Don't let me sneeze the virus of my gossip on you. If I finish my story, you will be infected with my perspective. It will change how you think about Beth. It will change how you think about me. It. Will. Change. How. You. Think! To complicate the dynamic, remember, I am not telling the whole story.

This will not be a comfortable 30 seconds. The first time you do this, it will be downright awkward. The second time, much more manageable. By the third time, you will almost be giddy. It works. It is the right thing to do.

But let's get real: Sometimes you *want* to hear what I have to say about Beth. She is kind of weird. She chews too loudly, she drives a Prius, wears Crocs and has bangs in the front and a bad perm in the back. She wears mismatched plaid and pleated denim. Good gawd! Who does that? She is two gallons of weird in a three-gallon bucket. So you are interested in what I have to say. And you're bored, or irritated, or thirsty, or tired, or the Wi-Fi is slow, or the President just annoyed you. Or you want me to like you. Whatever. You're interested. So you listen.

And my preface got your attention: "I really need help. I'm frustrated, and you're the only one who can help me." That made you feel pretty good. So you lean in. If you interrupt me with a "Wait…," it's just so you can go get popcorn and settle into a comfortable chair for the drama that is about to unfold. Honestly, it is sometimes fun to hear about people's drama. Well, not for *you* of course, but you have a *friend* who likes to hear it.

When we see triangulation for what it is, including its impact on us as the First Listener, we are more motivated to deal with it directly. When we have lived through the clutter and messes it creates, we are more driven to say, "This is triangulation. You need to talk directly to her. If you need help after that, I'd be willing to talk with both of you."

Of course, if you send me off to talk with Beth directly, I won't do it. I'll find someone else to speak with. But, here's the key, if the culture of our team reinforces direct communication and abstains from triangulation, I will be left with a choice: Communicate directly or build a bridge and get over it.

As a Supervisor, sometimes the triangulation/problem-solving line can blur. When a team member wants to talk and drifts into triangulating, simply interrupt with the question, "Have you spoken directly with Beth about this?" Then lean over, dial her extension and ask her to join you. This usually results in rapid editing on the part of the Triangulater.

> *All effective teams communicate directly. All of them. All. Of. Them. All effective Supervisors foster direct communication. All of them. All. Of. Them. You get the idea.*

> **Resilient Supervisory Skill #19: Break the Triangles and practice direct communication.**

Performance Management Tool 3: What? What? What?

As a supervisory leader, you may have come to believe that your value raises based on the number of accurate answers you dispense. You and your team have come to think of yourself as Google. If they ask a question, your experiential search engine of a brain goes into hyperdrive and returns a list of mostly helpful answers. Then, after selecting the best answer to their question, the team member turns and walks away. The line forms and you repeat the process for the bulk of your day.

You may also have heard that the best leaders have an "open door"[34] philosophy, so you strive to appear open, accessible and supportive. Until it's just too much. When you answer the same question several times, or when you answer questions that can easily be answered by just clicking on a link or opening a notebook or pausing for three seconds and thinking your frustration mounts.

You are not Google. You are not a vending machine of expired and calorie-dense answers. Your job is to ensure that the team performs better this week than it did last week; to ensure that the individual's performance is better today than yesterday. Your job is about one thing: performance. You are not a referee, not a police officer, not a therapist or kindly grandparent. You are in this job so that you and your team get stuff done… better this week than last… better next week than this week.

Since this is true, what do effective Supervisors do with questions, especially problems and challenges that they suspect the front-line employee has the ability and resources to deal with themselves? The three steps described in the Point of Leverage below are very effective. Try them out.

---

34 Even though very few Supervisors actually have doors to close, but you get my point.

> **Resilient Supervisory Skill #20: Use the What, What, What tool this week.**

Point of Leverage

When approached by a team member with a problem to solve, and you think they should be able to solve it, take the *What, What, What* approach by asking these three questions:

One: What problem are you trying to solve?

Most of the time, the problem a person brings to you is not the problem that needs to be solved. There is something that created this problem, and that is what deserves our attention.

Two: What have you done so far?

Three: What would you do if I were not available?

Using this approach helps you teach the employee how to solve problems and reinforces your expectations. It takes a little longer than merely giving her the answers (Google is quite fast), but it develops her ability to solve problems and take advantage of opportunities in the future.

Performance Management Tool 4: The SLY Model

When diagnosing a problem, apply the SLY model. This tool provides a disciplined way of addressing challenges at their roots.

In organizations of varying levels of complexity, the source of problems that result in poor performance arises from three thematic sources: structure, leadership or you (the individual). Imagine a very inexpensive combination lock. If you're lucky, you may open it on the first turn. If not, then the second turn. Occasionally, it will take a third attempt before the lock falls open.

Most (nearly 80%) of the problems we face arise because the structure we built created the problem. Structure refers to everything we have put in place to get our work done. It is how we've arranged our world. It is software, hardware, policy, procedure, tools, habits, norms, traditions, contracts, and schedules. It is put in place to solve problems and, if it works, it remains and becomes invisible. It governs and shapes our work almost entirely. Like habits, structure operates just below our awareness. Structure nudges us to think, feel and behave in specific, repetitive ways.

Most structure was put in place to solve specific problems without thought about long term impacts. In our study of the administrative processes in a large mechanical engineering firm, for example, we discovered that nearly 90% of them had nothing to do with the company's strategic plan. Some, in fact, were even at odds with the stated goals of the company. These processes were invisible examples of structure.[35]

Over time, even well-intentioned and widely accepted structure can create other problems.

A large regional hospital instituted a software-based acuity system designed, in part, to measure the complexity of a patient's treatment and adjust staffing to contend with a more demanding load. The new software replaced a tried-and-true paper system and "rules of thumb" used by seasoned Charge Nurses.

The new system could only be used from desktop computers at the nurse's station and not from the patients' room. Complete, detailed input for each patient at the beginning of every shift took eleven minutes

---

[35] In an attempt to increase professional billable hours from 65% of hours worked to 95% of hours worked, the coding structure (the antiquated process by which professionals tracked their time and coded it to specific projects) took nearly 10 minutes per hour to complete. Do the math: structure made it impossible to get more than 84% billable productivity. Therefore, in a vain attempt to attain billable goals, some of the engineers resorted to "creative accounting."

with the section containing information pertinent to staffing levels only accessible during the last 60 seconds of the task.

A shorter version of the process was optional, requiring only two minutes to complete, but it defaulted the patient's complexity (acuity) to a low level. This default was invisible to the nursing staff.

Nurses were busy because of patient load (number of patients) and acuity (complexity of care). Busy nurses look for safe ways to save steps and minutes. The structure defaulted to information that created staffing models for less busy, less complex care. Busy nurses skipped the longer reporting options. Staffing models consistently scheduled far fewer nurses than required. Busy nurses got busier. Performance slipped.

This is an example of structure creating a performance problem. Well-trained and well-intentioned nurses began to perform poorly. Patient care slipped. Conflict between nurses and administrative (staffing) teams increased. Structure—how they arranged their world to get their work done—was the problem.

Eventually, a team addressed the problem by designing a 45-second input process that addressed acuity levels first. Staffing increased when needed and decreased when not. Workload balanced out. Care improved. Nurses smiled a little more.

Identify what part of the performance challenge is happening as a result of structure. Change the structure, and watch the problem disappear. Usually.

If the problem remains after the structure has changed, Leaders (the L in the SLY model) need to clarify expectations. After structural causes, unclear expectations from leaders are the next most significant source of problems and account for up to 15% of performance deficits at work. Problems that flow from unclear leadership expectations have an outsized impact on the organization.

> *Problems arising from unclear expectations from leaders have a massive impact on the organization.*

Once Leaders have clarified expectations, and once structure is elegant, clear and efficient, all that is left is the individual. You (the individual) account for only about 5% of the performance problems we see at work. To put it another way, only 5% of the time is the individual (You) the only problem. When performance problems occur, 95% of the time the individual is doing what the structure supports (or requires) and thinks they are meeting the (unclear) expectations of their Leaders.

> *Here's the rub: 100% of the time, problems become visible because the individual does something wrong. So it looks like the individual is the problem all of the time.*

I guarantee if you replace the individual without changing the Structure and clarifying Leadership expectations, the problem will happen again.

Leo and Linda

Leo was a Supervisor in a call center for three years before he was fired for sleeping on the job. He was counseled, coached, disciplined. He stayed awake. For three months.[36] Then his napping returned. When confronted, he said he wasn't sleeping but just thinking. And his eyes were dry. So he closed them. When his snores could be heard 20 feet away,[37] his description of the behavior resonated less than his soft palate.

It was only after he was fired that another Supervisor, over a beer with Leo, helped identify a cause for the noon naps. Recently married, Leo and his wife both worked grave yard shifts. They liked it. They arranged their friendships, transportation, recreation, household chores,

---

36 My editor suggested I re-write this sentence. But I think it's funny, so I left it alone. Of course, he didn't stay awake for three months. He just didn't fall asleep *at work* for a three-month period.

37 Apparently, some people make that rhythmic, rumbling noise when in deep thought.

diet, exercise and time together around the graveyard lifestyle. They were in hog heaven. (Or Vampire heaven, since it was graveyard shift.)

A new approach to supervisory schedules did not allow for shift-bids based on seniority but required shift rotations every six months. Leo rotated from his beloved graveyard shift to day shift. His wife's job at another organization did not allow her to change her schedule. Leo and Linda (let's call her Linda because that's her name) set about cramming all the details of life into this new reality leaving Leo with three hours of sleep on most nights.

All the energy drinks and Peanut M&Ms in the vending machine could not stave off the gravitational pull of exhaustion and the march of melatonin during the slowest, dullest part of the day shift, and Leo succumbed to napping on his feet.

When confronted with this behavior he would redouble his effort to stay awake and "try harder" (a classic approach to dealing with a structural problem masquerading as a *You-are-the-Problem* problem) and failed. Epically. Though none of his naps were of the hour-long variety, merely sleeping for three minutes made him the source of mockery. And the recipient of an unemployment check.

Had Leo been able to look at the structure of his life first, rather than into the bottom of a Monster Energy can, he would likely still be employed as a Supervisor.

I am in no way suggesting abdication of the responsibility Leo bore for his naps. We are all responsible for our own behavior and our underlying disciplines and habits. And I am not suggesting that we are free to outsource our responsibility by blaming the structure, or unclear leadership expectations for that matter. I am, however, pointing the way to a solution.

Use the SLY approach. When a problem presents itself (usually through the symptom of individual behavior), look first at the structure in which the behavior occurs. Changes there will leverage any changes in leadership expectations and enable sustained and effective personal behavior choices. Regardless of how egregious the individual's behaviors, look first to structure. Look there, not as a way of excusing personal behavior, but rather as a way of ensuring traction when the personal behavior changes.

> **Resilient Supervisory Skill #21: Practice using the SLY approach to problem solving.**

Performance Management Tool 5: The Skill of Tipping

Tipping is the skill of focusing on the individual and not on other people. It enables you to sift through the noise of a conversation, to overcome distraction and defensiveness, and to address a core problem. It is an incredibly easy, and powerful, supervisory tool.

It is time to sit down and speak with a team member about her performance. You've watched her quality and engagement dip over the last week or so and decide to talk to her about what you have observed. A few moments into the conversation, as you describe her behavior, she interrupts saying that her coworker, Rhonda, has been doing the same thing, but longer. Distracted, you want to ask for details.

Now is the time to employ the "tipping "method. Listen for just a brief moment and then interject, "But that's not what we're here to talk about. We're here to talk about you."

This is tipping. It's as simple as that.

If a member of your team tries to tip the conversation away from the topic, in this case, her performance, tip the conversation back by saying, "Ok, but that's not what we're here to talk about."

Be careful when tipping to not make any promises. For example, do not say, "Ok, I will look into that and get back to you." Also, be careful not to imply agreement by nodding or tacitly agreeing just so you don't appear rude. Simply take the conversation back to the point of the discussion at hand. "But we are here to talk about you."

Practice this a time or two with someone who is not at work so you can get familiar with it.[38] Then, if any significant issues come up, simply make a mental note and deal with it later.

If the distracting issue relates to the employee with whom you are talking, suggest that you put it aside for now, and then return to it in another conversation. Avoid adding topics to the conversation. Save it for later.

You may need to tip the conversation back to the issue at hand multiple times. Stay calm and respectful, but just keep doing it until you have addressed what you set out to talk about.

> **Resilient Supervisory Skill #22: Practice Tipping the conversation back to the issue at hand whenever someone becomes distracted by other seemingly related problems.**

Performance Management Tool 6: The OIC Model

When performance according to the standard dips, use the OIC Model of communication. The O represents Observed Behavior. The I represents the Interpretation (or meaning) I give the behavior. The C represents the Consequence of Behavior with that Interpretation. The OIC model is easy and very effective.

This skill may take a few practice laps to perfect, not because of its difficulty, but because of the speed of your brain. You think so quickly, even when thinking slowly, that this approach may take some practiced concentration. Your mind will leap from Observed Behavior to the

---

[38] If you have ankle-biters at home, they are a wonderful real-time lab in which to learn this skill. Do not, however, attempt this with your spouse. Or, for that matter, this with a Sheriff's Deputy after he pulls you over for speeding. "I know, but the reason we are here is to talk about why you feel you need to pull someone over who is going with the flow of traffic." This may not end well. Remember, use the right tool for the right job. Just sayin'.

Interpretation of the behavior at light speed, register your Interpretation (the meaning you give the behavior) as fact, and proceed from that point as though you had discovered some hidden secret.

Let me illustrate. Imagine I am sitting with you at a table right now, along with three other people. You present an idea to the group. A few seconds into your presentation, I fold my arms across my chest, lean back in the chair, purse my lips, frown, shake my head slightly and look out the window. I do all of this in two or three seconds. What do you think? What did you observe? Don't read on… Stop and say aloud what you think.

You thought what most people would think. What everyone would think, to be frank. "What's *his* problem? What a jerk! He doesn't like my idea. He hates my idea. I feel judged. He must think I'm stupid." This is your *Interpretation* of the Behavior you *Observed*. In a flash, your limbic system and its superhero partner, the reticular activating system, combined forces like Power Rangers and locked on the threat created by the interpretation of my behavior.

You *observed* my folded arms, my frown and the shake of my head. You did *not observe disapproval*. You observed hands, eyes, lips, shoulders, and chair. You *interpreted* those *observed behaviors as disapproval*. You gave them their meaning. But because of your speed of thought, and of the need for mental efficiency when under threat, your mind compressed *observations and interpretations* into one thing: in this case, disapproval.

Once we have an *interpretation* (this process takes one or two seconds), our curious mind begins to make connections with other such interpretations and, unsurprisingly, predicts Consequences. This Observe, Interpret, Consequence loop speeds up and yields a conclusion. *What a judgmental jerk! He is going to resist my idea, and I will need to work harder to succeed.* Then, just that fast, you've put me into a category out of which I will not easily climb. This categorization occurs much more efficiently when you think of my behavior as threatening than when you infer friendly intentions.

Let's take your fast brain to work. James is late by five minutes. Well, he is late/early; he is "L'early."[39] His shift starts at 7am, and you like it when the team arrives at 6:45 or earlier. It's not written down but expected all the same. James enters at 6:58, spills his coffee in the hall, rushes to clean it up, makes it to the morning meeting, coat still on, with a fresh cup, and sits down at precisely 7:04. With a deep sigh, he settles in, reads the room and then asks a question that's already been answered.

What did you observe?
Careful. What did you *observe*?

Perhaps you are a fast learner. You *observed* only what was written above. If that was your response, you nailed it.

Second question: What could the Observed Behavior mean (its Interpretation)? Here's the fun part. It could mean a lot of things. The least likely meaning is that he is resisting your expectation, refuses to be a team player and selfishly decided to make everyone, including you (especially you), miserable. Selfish little bitch!

I'm a bit dramatic for effect. This is how our mind works, especially when we are inattentive and tired. It's just more efficient to glue *Observation* together with *Interpretation* and think of it as reality.

Here's my recommendation: When you observe behavior that is outside of your expectations, mention the behavior (just the behavior) to the team member. Then sit there and look at him. That's it. He will explain the behavior's meaning. If not, simply ask what it means. Change the I in OIC from Interpretation to Inquiry. Rather than make up your own mind about the behavior, just ask him what it means.

---

39 L'early: a term used to describe someone who shows up precisely seconds before he must be somewhere, usually disorganized and frazzled, and requires 20 minutes to settle in before the start time, causing a distraction as the rest of the team waits for his drama to subside. And he is always L'*early*.

Observed behavior
Inquiry (ask what it means)
Confirm (where do we go next?)

"James, I noticed that you rushed into the meeting today after we had already started." Then stop talking! Just look at him without a scowl or frown or whiff of superiority. Just wait.

James will respond. His response will be 1.) An explanation, 2.) Surprise at your observation which he didn't even make of himself, 3.) Or a, "Yeah. So?" All these responses are straightforward to address. If he explains, listen, nod and repeat your expectation to him, including why it's important (see the "so that" connector). Then move on.

If he is surprised and unaware, listen, nod and repeat your expectation. If he is defensive and terse, listen, nod, and repeat your behavioral expectations, including the connection to why.

Then ask, "Let's confirm: We are all here and ready to go 15 to 20 minutes before the meeting. That's my expectation. What will you do differently next time?"

If he responds with, "I'll try harder," say, "I assume you are already trying hard. Other than that, what will you do differently next time?"

This is a crucial moment in performance and expectation management. Do not disengage until he has described what he will do differently. Include a time stamp. "When will you do it? When will we touch base again about it?" Then put it on your calendar right in front of him. And, when the time comes, follow up.

This simple, often very brief, conversation is the heart of all performance management work.

Resilient Supervisory Skill #23: Practice separating Observed Behavior from what you think the behavior means.

Performance Management Tool 7: The Myth of the Right Time

You are a nice person, or at least you play one on TV. You don't micromanage and detest it when it has been done to you. Add these together with a good dose of busy-ness, and you may wait too long to address missed expectations or performance problems. You may, like most Supervisors, want to wait to see if a pattern develops then address the problem as a pattern rather than an isolated incident. You may wait until you have enough examples to "make a case" and hope for the "right time" to deal with missed expectations or sloppy performance.

This is a problem. When we wait for a pattern to develop, and for our schedule to clear, and for their schedule to clear, and for the perfect alignment of Rock Star Energy drinks and mood, we've waited too long. Talking to a team member about missed expectations under these circumstances only erodes trust. If you've seen the problem for weeks, and are just now addressing it, it is natural for your team member to wonder what else is lying in wait, undeveloped but still disappointing.

Waiting for a pattern to develop, while it seems kind now, is quite unkind later. It leaves the employee wondering if you are always watching and waiting for him to mess up. The clinical term for that dynamic is "icky."

Skilled and respectful Supervisors address performance problems missed expectations and inappropriate behavior immediately. They make the right moment happen out of thin air. They discuss the issue with curiosity and respect, but they discuss it without delay.

And let's get real, performance management conversations are very short. Three minutes of well-constructed conversation changes a lot. If your conversation goes much longer, you've waited too long, are overly concerned with your feelings (or theirs) or are delivering a long list of problems gathered over weeks or months.

Most Supervisors imagine performance management conversations as long drawn-out affairs, so they wait until they have time and energy to have them. This is faulty thinking. Make them short, sweet and to the point.

Look at your watch. Now, imagine identifying a performance problem, clarifying expectations, making a simple plan for next steps, all in 60 seconds. Try it. Imagine that the employee is curious and asks a couple questions. You answer, tip the conversation back to the point at hand, and consume another 30 seconds. You smile, say thanks and move on. 90 seconds. Practice it.

Put yourself in the position of the one receiving the message about missed expectations or poor performance. Imagine sitting down with your Supervisor and, after some uncomfortable small talk, listening to a list of issues, with supporting dates and times, presented as examples of a larger theme of ineffectiveness. You would be justified in your embarrassment and irritation. You would be correct in wondering what else the Supervisor is tracking, waiting long enough to build an irrefutable case. The distance created between a team member and team leader by this approach is difficult to bridge.

If you notice a missed expectation, address it now. Address it using the OIC Model. Address it with humble curiosity. Remind yourself and the team member of your expectations. Don't wait for the forces of nature and psychology and Oprah reruns to align.

Remind the team member of the standard, along with the behavioral expectations it takes to meet that standard. As mentioned above, high, clear performance standards are your best friend. Remember that standards are completely within our behavioral control and supported with systems and structures. Goals, on the other hand, are partially within our control. We expect complete compliance with a standard. We expect an incremental, timely movement towards a goal. Knowing the difference between a goal and a standard will set you free and liberate your team.

Once past initial training expect those you supervise to meet standards every time. Expect them to achieve goals most of the time. Working well with other Supervisors is a goal. Direct communication, rather than insipid triangulation, is a standard. Reading this book in a week is a goal. Filling out time sheets by the 20th is a standard. You get the idea. At least, that's my goal.

Showing up on time is a standard. Showing up early is a goal. Spelling correctly is a standard. Using descriptive grammar (compared to prescriptive grammar) is a goal. Reviewing every work-related email before shift's end is a standard. Remembering what was communicated is a goal.

Knowing the difference is crucial. Treating a standard like it is a goal will only lead to complex personnel problems down the (short) road. Handling goals like standards will only lead to a demoralized team.[40]

Stephanie was a new Supervisor who observed an experienced telephone customer service rep curse, unplug his headset, push back

---

[40] A word to the Perfectionist Reader: This difference between goals and standards lies at the heart of perfectionism. To the perfectionist, everything is a standard. Lighten up, friend. Some things are standards. Most are goals. Take a deep breath and learn the difference. It will set you free. (From one OCPT to another. Obsessive, Compulsive, Perfectionistic Twit.)

from the console, and spout frustration at the number of stupid callers today. The entire floor heard the rant, as did the IT guys down the hall. And the UPS guy.

Within five minutes, Stephanie approached the team member. "I understand your frustration, but I expect that you don't make it worse by broadcasting your emotions to the entire team."

He replied, "You're one to talk! You used to do this all the time!"

Stephanie responded, "You are correct. I did. And I was wrong every time I did it. And I will not do it again in this role. I expect that you do not voice your frustration on the floor again. Frustration will most definitely happen again. Therefore, we have breaks. Take a break if possible. Leave the floor for a few minutes, compose yourself and return."

I overheard another Supervisor, accused in a similar situation, defend her past behavior as somehow different. I could not help but feel that she lost some of her credibility by doing so.

Avoid diluting the standard because you had a difficult time meeting it when you were in their position. Standards are easy for some people to meet; difficult for others. Perhaps you had a difficult time consistently meeting a specific standard (and complained about it to others). Since it was challenging, you may have even found yourself disagreeing with its value even while others met it easily.

Now that you are a Supervisor you may give a free pass to others who struggle similarly. If you do, it is not a standard. And you will be seen as unjustly favoring one person over another.

Important things must never be left unsaid. The annoying airport message applies: If you see something, say something. This relates to both standards and goals. When a team member who has struggled meeting a standard finally shifts gears and now consistently meets the standard, say something. When she meets a goal, say something. When someone moves closer to a goal, say something. When an entire team meets the standards consistently after a particularly challenging day, say something.

In the busy-ness of the day, it is easy to convince yourself that your observations are best left for later. And later becomes next month. The impact of an observation made in September but communicated in October is rarely what we expect. And it often backfires.

> **The Resilient Supervisor Skill #24: Do it now.**

Look in the Mirror

If imagining yourself using any of these performance management tools makes you feel uncomfortable, ask yourself why. Often our discomfort arises from a faulty assumption about our role as a supervisory leader. We are leaders with supervisory responsibility primarily focused on accomplishing the mission through our team by supporting continual improvement.

We are not family. We are not besties. We are leaders. The people we serve deserve our best, unselfish efforts.

Chapter 19:

Your Calendar is Your Most Powerful Tool

I cannot overemphasize the power of the calendar. Put everything on your calendar. And make sure you only have one calendar. There's only one you, and you can just do one thing at a time, so just use one calendar. Allow others to have access to your calendar digitally, but no one can put anything on your calendar without your permission.[41]

When you've decided what is essential in your day, week, month, and a request is made that interrupts the most important investments of your time, resist the temptation to explain, and simply say, "I have another commitment."

Highly effective people establish a cadence for commitments. They set aside regular time to reach out to the future and protect time for the most important things.

On most Sunday Evenings, for example, I look at the week ahead and identify the single most important thing I need to accomplish that

---

41 You may be one of those rare birds that has assistance with your calendar. If so, put commitments on your calendar through that person. You'll save yourself the frustration and embarrassment of committing to two or three things at once.

week. At the beginning of each day, I decide the single most important task or conversation or decision I need to make or complete for that day. And, by the way, I complete these commitments to myself before going to sleep at night. It is a promise I make to myself. Since I fulfill these promises, regardless of the cost, I am careful about making commitments. This discipline has helped me leverage my time more than anything I have ever learned as an adult.

Delaying decisions about potential commitments is sometimes the best approach. If you do not have enough information and if the decision does not need to be made now, delay it. But put the time to make the decision on your calendar.

You can also extend your effectiveness by not making decisions that belong to someone else. Avoid making decisions that are not yours to make. This is easy to apply when the decision is above you in the organization. But it is more difficult when the decision comes from below. When a member of your team asks you a question, he is often asking you to decide about something he is fully capable and responsible for deciding on his own.

The Principle of One

What one thing are you trying to accomplish? Do it once. Have one conversation. Make one call. Write one email. Touch mail once. Touch documents once. Avoid the "for now" pile. Every resilient and effective leader I've known is exceptional at this skill. They are also very good at focusing, during any given block of time, on only one thing. They do not multitask and flit back and forth between shallow distractions in vain hope that those small tasks will all add up to significance.[42]

---

42 Multitasking is a myth. The human brain can consciously focus on only one thing at a time. While we can hold three or four things at the edges of our attention, we can only focus on one. It is neurologically impossible to focus on more. Therefore, those who claim to be multitaskers are actually multi-switchers: they switch between tasks quickly. Multiple studies have demonstrated a 50% decrease in quality and productivity when we switch between just two focus points.

YOUR CALENDAR IS YOUR MOST POWERFUL TOOL

Simplify your life. It brings huge benefits. Decide what clothes you like to wear to work in advance and stick with that decision. Turn it into a uniform of sorts. Eat the same simple breakfast every day. Have a morning routine that is the same. Leave at the same time. Arrive ten minutes early. Slowly walk into work. Communicate with one person (directly) about the issue at hand. That one person is the one who can solve the problem or take charge of the opportunity. Have one calendar. Put everything on your calendar (once). Have one to-do list. Meal prep for work-week meals once at the beginning of the week.

Make sure every commitment you agree to fits your job and career objectives and that you have time to do it. "Let me check my calendar" is the best response to any request. Then see if you have time and put… it… on… your… calendar. Never agree to something that doesn't go on your calendar. This discipline alone will make you significantly more effective and resilient. Calendaring forces reality into optimism. It forces us to think, even if imprecisely, about how long something will take. Calendaring nearly always forces a value judgement as it prompts me to choose between what I've already committed to (including time off) and the new, sparkly opportunity in front of me.

The discipline of the calendar forces me to slow my racing mind and make intentional value-based decisions.

Highly effective Supervisors also learn to slow their mind, focus on the person, conversation, task before them, listen intently, learn or decide and then move on. Counterintuitively, when we slow our mind and focus on the present, we are at least 30% more productive than when we hurry through the day.

Insight always occurs in moments when our mind is calm, open, curious, relaxed and unafraid. In an upcoming book (titled *Eureka! Preparing Your Mind for Insight at Work and at Play*),[43] I highlight recent

---

[43] I've long been fascinated by the value of moments of true insight that I've experienced and benefitted from in others. This book explores the current neuropsychological connections and the disciplines required to create more of these moments especially when faced with complex challenges and opportunities.

discoveries in neuropsychology that explain why a calm, open, unafraid and curious mind is the garden of insight. I describe why leaders and influencers in High-Impact organizations need to cultivate the disciplines required to gain and recognize a true insight.

One of the surprising discoveries in this research is the presence of a calendaring discipline. It has the immediate effect of prioritizing and organizing investments of time, sifting between urgent and noisy demands to find essential and leveraged work. The byproduct of this discipline is a less worried mind. The connection between a focused, unhurried, unafraid and unworried mind and applied judgement arising from insight is a powerful one.

If you find yourself feeling busy all the time, overworked and occasionally distracted, and if your default answer to a new opportunity is, "I don't have time," this exercise will benefit you.

Take note of how you *actually* spend your time. Track it for two or three weeks. Be ruthless and accurate. Track every minute of every day for at least 14 days. Group your time spent into distinct categories. Be utterly honest. No one else will see the results. Include how much time you spend doing everything.

You track your money, why not track your time as well.[44] Then see what that time log reveals. You may be surprised. It will also help you understand where time leaks occur. It may even shock you to discover that you spent seven hours on Facebook. Or twelve hours watching television. This awareness of how you spend your time will be very enlightening.

Then take control of your time. Intentionally budget it weekly, in advance of the week, according to the few things that really matter to you.

---

[44] People who track their money fall into two categories: Those who track money BEFORE they spend it and those who track their money AFTER they spend it. The BEFORE-Trackers are better at tracking their time, at budgeting it intentionally. They are also far less stressed.

YOUR CALENDAR IS YOUR MOST POWERFUL TOOL

The more responsibility you have, the less your time merely is "your time." Other people have claim to your time as your career progresses. This means that the minutes and hours over which you have stewardship must be even more carefully stewarded.

This discipline yields surprising freedom. I know that every hour I spend is given in support of something that matters. Like a mighty locomotive, I am free… if I have tracks.

> **The Resilient Supervisor Skill #25: Use your Calendar for Everything. Decide how you will use your time well before you use it.**

Chapter 20:

He's NOT a Good Engineer

"But he's such a good software engineer. He can code like no one I've ever seen."

I've lost track of how many times I've heard this sentence over the years. It has several versions: he's such a good designer, or developer, or welder, or salesman, or HR specialist. Replace Engineer with any profession, and the sentence is likely one you've heard before. It usually follows a long and detailed description of the frustrations the Supervisor has with a team member. It is as though being exceptional at one part of one's job and horrible at other parts is good enough. It is the professional version of "Bless his heart" heard in conversation over sweet tea in South Carolina or Mississippi.[45]

He shows up late, gossips throughout the work day, refuses to learn anything that is not mandated, treats certain other team members with

---

[45] We feel bad about expressing our frustrations with other people and try to balance the bitter observations with a little sweetness. The Southern United States comment "Bless his heart" comes in other forms as well: But he's a nice guy. But I really like her. He's special. Or, my favorite, Just Sayin', which is used throughout this book.

disdain while holding others in high regard, rudely interacts when a customer calls with a "stupid" question, and complains loudly that the new Software Engineers will never be as good as he is.

But he's such a good Engineer.

He attends mandatory training, sits in the back of the room, with arms folded, scowling throughout the session. When asked for his input in the class, he refuses to engage, other than with muttered complaints about wasting his precious time. New team members are told they must endure his negative, bitter personality like some strange rite of passage. Everyone had to deal with him, so the newbie has to as well. It's just part of the job. Get used to it.

But he's such a good Engineer.

He never commits big technical mistakes, at least not ones he's admitted to making. He knows the dark arts of coding and understands the tricks of the network better than anyone. He has a long history and knowledge that predates most people in the organization. He knows how to deliver projects on time. He has been doing the job so long that his intuition about potential problems is downright spooky. When the phone rings, he knows on the first ring if it is a real problem with a customer or just a complaint from Gladys Kravitz.[46]

But, let's be clear, he is failing at his job.

High-Impact organizations are staffed at every level by professionals. Even jobs that were formerly considered clerical, low-level, low-skill now require the proficiency of a professional.

Professionals are highly effective in three arenas. They are, of course, effective in the technical aspects of their job. But that is not enough to be regarded as a professional. They must also be effective in the training

---

[46] Played by Alice Pierce from 1964-1966 on the TV Show *Bewitched*, Gladys Kravitz was the nosy, hyper-observant neighbor who saw every strange event across the street at the home of Darren and Samantha Stevens. She would freak out and scream for her husband Abner in every episode. By the time Abner came to the window, the bizarre event across the street had ended, leaving him to question his wife's sanity.

HE'S NOT A GOOD ENGINEER

segment of their job. And they are exceptional team members.

The graphic below illustrates the balanced expert. It is a model that is true of every professional, regardless of the career. The T-3 model has proven to be helpful for Supervisors who deal with the "good Engineer" dynamic.

Pie chart divided into three sections: Teamwork, Technological Competence, Training.

Technical aspects, when mastered, make a person appear professional, but only when working alone or with other experienced professionals who require little interaction. Mastering the skills that require precise compliance with standards while simultaneously applying judgement is the hallmark of a true professional in any environment.

Professionals also assume that the context in which their technical skills are practiced will change. This requires an enormous and perpetual appetite for learning. The professional is the driver for his own development. Even though the organization can provide an opportunity for some training, the professional realizes that this is not enough. He assumes responsibility for his personal training so that he stays on the cutting edge of excellence. He studies during and after hours. He searches for others who can sharpen his skills. He looks down the road and predicts the skills he will need in the future, and he begins working on them now.

Professionals are voracious learners. They are dynamic experts. Static experts, in contrast, have attained expertise in a specific arena and maintained it over the years. If that expertise is valued, they are secure.

> *Dynamic Experts are different. They gained expertise in a specific arena, then another. After a short time, they realized that their value as a professional exists, not because they are good at something, but because they are good at getting good. This is what I call a dynamic expert. This is a professional.*

Lastly, all professionals function in highly connected environments. There are no solo practitioners of a profession. Therefore, they need to be able to work in a group of other highly committed people with diverse experience and talents. Sometimes they lead. Sometimes they follow. Sometimes they are part of a team, and sometimes they lead the team. That shift in position can occur daily. All professionals are good at working with and through other people; at building, working in and leading teams when called on to do so.

Together, these three arenas of effectiveness combine to make a professional. Leave one of them out, and he is not a professional.

So no, he's not a good Engineer. At best, he is good at one third of his job. He is failing at his job. And it is possible that he is the only one who does not know it.

When evaluating yourself or others, use the T-3 Model of Professionalism. Start by identifying the critical skills necessary in each area. Then add the important skills. Finally, add the highly desirable skills. That third level describes the professional. Use that model to create conversations, evaluations, coaching and even discipline. Use the model for yourself and your Supervisory Team. It will be exceptionally revealing.

Teamwork

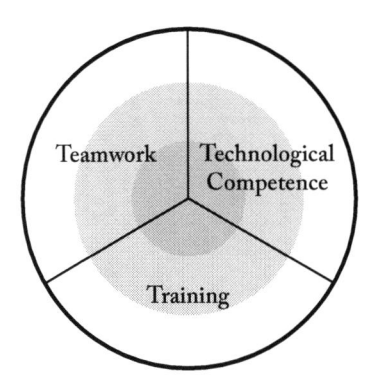

Technological Competence

Training

Resilient Supervisory Skill #26: Become a Pro and expect Professionalism out of your Team Members using the T-3 Model.

Chapter 21:

Tips for Becoming and Remaining a Resilient Supervisor (and a Healthy Team Member)

By now it has no doubt occurred to you that the job of Supervisor is hard on your body. It is also likely occurred to you that if you have a lot of energy and are healthy, the job is much easier to do. Your physical health will make becoming an exceptional Supervisor much easier. The good news is your physical health is mostly up to you.

As with all small investments made over a long period, something I like to call the compound effect, making small changes and sticking to them over a long period will pay off enormously.

How do effective Supervisors, especially in environments and jobs like yours, manage their physical health? They manage their health by being careful about their diet, their sleep, and their physical exercise. They also manage their health by being attentive to address conflict when it is small so they can discuss it in a productive, low-impact fashion.

Most Supervisors in High-Impact organizations will benefit from a simple Mediterranean diet.[47] The Mediterranean diet is one of the most effective ways to eat if you are a Supervisor.

It is also important to pay attention to the impact of shift work on your diet. If you are a Supervisor in an organization that requires you to work different shifts, the effects on your body are significant. The most current research indicates that those people who work off-shift hours, for example, swing shift or graveyard, slow their basic metabolic rate and begin to crave calorie-dense foods high in sugar and usually processed. Coincidentally, these foods are readily available in most work places.

Resilient Supervisors manage their sleep. If you are one of the Supervisors whose schedule changes frequently, this will be a challenge. If, however, you have a very static schedule, you will likely be able to manage your sleep a little bit better.

Some tips for managing your sleep: Use blackout shades that keep all the light out of your room. Use a white noise generator such as a fan or a digital device or app to fall asleep. Stop using all digital devices 45 to 60 minutes before going to bed. Avoid the blue light from digital screens altogether for that same period.

Set two alarms. Don't drink alcohol two hours before going to sleep. Don't drink anything one hour before going to sleep. Lower the temperature in the room, if possible, to around 60°. Manage what you think about as you fall asleep. Focusing on what you're grateful for as you fall asleep is one of the most effective ways to set yourself up for deep and restful sleep.

Do a personal sleep study. Discover how much sleep you need. The best way to do this is, over a four- or five-day period, set your alarm to

---

[47] The Mediterranean Diet follows the diets of those living in Greece, Southern Italy and some parts of Spain, especially in the mid-20th century. The diet includes proportionally high consumption of olive oil, unrefined cereals, vegetables and fruits, along with legumes. It also includes fish, a moderate amount of cheese, yogurt, and wine. I have looked far and wide and failed to find a version of this diet that includes Scotch, especially my beloved Laphroaig 15 year. Deep sigh.

go off nine hours after you go to bed. Then notice when you wake up. The first day you may wake up with the alarm. The second day you will likely wake up before the alarm. Test it again for the third day. If you find that you wake up at seven hours and twenty minutes of sleep three days in a row, then you are a person who likely needs seven-and-a-half hours of sleep. If you find yourself waking up at eight hours and forty-five minutes, then you are probably a person who needs that much sleep. The trick is to make sure you go to bed with enough time to fall asleep and sleep for the time your body needs. This requires an immense amount of discipline.

Like diet, sleep is one of the most effective ways to increase your abilities as a Supervisor. The people you supervise deserve to have a rested and healthy Supervisor.

Some People Adapt and Stay Healthy

A percentage of Supervisors in High-Impact organizations are physically healthy, not burnt out, and adapt to change well. They are careful, from the start of their careers, to manage their health for the long term. They manage their sleep. They get daily exercise.[48] They are careful about what they eat and drink (five or six days a week). They work hard and rarely bring work or worry about work home with them. They have intense interests outside of work.

They have strong relationships with people who are not at work and not part of their profession. They also have good relationships at work. They have a low entertainment-to-education consumption ratio (they consume media that educates much more frequently than media

---

48 Daily exercise for the rest of your life is the single biggest determining factor of longevity. This assumes you have a reasonable diet, such as the Mediterranean Diet, mentioned above. It is impossible to out-train a bad diet. If you are nearing 50 (or can see it in your rear-view mirror) I highly recommend *Younger Next Year*, Crowley and Lodge. This simple, profound book is instructive and inspiring. It's available on Amazon in Kindle, paperback and Audible formats.

that entertains). They think of tasks in two broad categories: creative tasks and consumptive tasks. They work at creating rather than always consuming.

Furthermore, they avoid drama at work like the plague. Consequently, they avoid dramatic people at work (and outside of work). They focus on learning and adapting quickly to change rather than on resisting it as "yet another change."

They are careful to manage their own assumptions and control their behaviors carefully. Overall, they take responsibility for their physical and emotional health because they know the job will slowly kill them if they don't.

> **Resilient Supervisory Skill #27: Manage your vitality every day, without fail, for the rest of your life.**

The Disciplines of Healthy High-Impact Supervisors

May I get personal? There are some physically healthy Supervisors in High-Impact organizations, specifically in high-tech and knowledge-based enterprises. The supervisory job, while not stressful every minute of every day, is not friendly to your body. From the first day on the job, the role and the environment (small and large) sets us up to become exceptionally unhealthy. Stress, sedentary work, indoor light settings, digital sensory saturation, internal team conflict, constant adjustments, fueled by fast-food diets all combine to create a mind-numbing body-thickening atmosphere.

Many high-tech, knowledge-based organizations are among the unhealthiest workplace environments in western economies. Our research reveals that new employees in these industries gain an average of five pounds in the first six months of employment and an additional four pounds every year of employment for the first five years. A 180-pound team member will be nearly 210 pounds in five years. That same study suggests he will be 230 pounds nearing his tenth anniversary. He will likely also have high blood pressure, high cholesterol and show signs of a pre-diabetic condition. And those in Supervisory roles in these organizations experience greater weight gain than those they supervise. Where do I sign up?

But you are not doomed. Not everyone will end up like this. Some have defied the odds and have remained healthy for years. How have they done it?

We have studied these people for over three decades. Here's what we've uncovered. Specifically, their disciplines look something like this:

They get 7.5 hours of sleep, managing their schedule and environment so that it is possible.

They begin each day with a routine that enhances focus and gratitude.[49]

They work out 30-45 minutes per day, six days a week, focusing on heart rate. They mix aerobic exercise with resistance training.

They limit alcohol consumption to one drink per day or two drinks two days a week.

They drink the ounces/day of water equivalent to half their weight. (75 ounces for a 150-pound person).

They eat a version of the Mediterranean diet, bringing their food to work and rarely ordering out.

They stand at work more than 50% of the time.

They walk away from drama (literally, they walk away).

They rarely talk about drama at work with friends or family members, preferring to engage in other topics.

They communicate directly at work rather than triangulate and prefer to address conflict quickly.

They volunteer to be the first to learn a new approach or new technology.

---

49 In *The Miracle Morning*, Hal Elrod describes an approach he calls Life SAVERS. S=Silence, A=Affirmations (gratitude), V=Visualization, E=Exercise, R=Reading (to learn), and S=Scribing (short journaling). His story is worth the read. The model is a version similar to one I've followed for nearly 30 years.

They change clothes when they get home and have specific clothes they wear only at work.[50]

They drink 2 to 3 cups of coffee per day, usually in the first quarter of their day, and never drink energy drinks.

They rarely eat candy or cookies or cake at work.

They do not smoke cigarettes.

Many engage in competitive activities outside of work.

They watch their "consume/create ratio" working to create beauty or value every day.

These disciplines eventually become a habit and result in a physically healthy lifestyle. Which of these were you able to say you regularly do?

---

50 Changing out of the clothes worn to work when you get home, along with washing your hands, creates a surprisingly effective psychological boundary between work and home. It is a symbolic way of completing the work cycle and represents "finishing" when most supervisory jobs are never ending.

Chapter 22:

Time to Multiply--Erickson's Stages of Life and the Lessons for Supervisory Leaders

Erik Erikson (1902-1994) was a psychological theorist and practitioner who diverted from some of Sigmund Freud's (1856-1939) controversial theories of development by suggesting that our social growth ideally progresses as we resolve eight psycho-social choices in a particular sequence.

The first five stages of development occur from birth through about 18 years of age. The last three from our early 20s through the end of life.

Stage one (Will I trust or mistrust?) is all about learning whom to trust. Stage two (Can I do it myself or do I doubt myself?) is about learning to be autonomous. Stage three (Can I overcome my limits with and through others?) is about taking the initiative. Stage four (Can I consistently plan and excel compared to others, or am I always inferior?) is about industry and achievement. Stage five (Who am I, and what do I want to be?) is about beginning to resolve role and identity.

Then, according to Erikson, we progress through three stages as adults. At this point, his theory becomes especially instructive to me and relative to our roles as supervisory leaders in High-Impact organizations.

The first stage of adulthood, he calls Intimacy vs. Isolation. In this stage, typically occurring from the early 20s through the early 40s, we have developed a strong sense of self and can, therefore, develop close, robust and lasting relationships on several levels. Highly effective leaders emerge from this stage sure of who they are, of what matters most to them, of their strengths and weaknesses and, if successful, with a hearty sense of humor. Supervisors who are unsure of their core values, competencies and skills emerge from their 30s insecure and isolated. Under pressure, they often fall prey to stronger personalities and are easily manipulated by others.

Those who emerge from this period with a strong sense of self are capable and resilient leaders. If you are a supervisory leader in your 30s, say "YES!" to every opportunity to lead that comes your way. Pay close attention to what you learn about yourself in these years. Journal regularly and let adversity and adventure shape you.

Erikson's second stage of adulthood is called Generativity vs. Stagnation and occurs in our 40s through or mid 60s (depending on vitality and health). This stage's primary challenge lies in answering the question "Will I take or will I give?"

Erikson postulates that taking leads to stagnation. The "I've paid my dues" and the "I deserve to coast" mindsets create a slow decline mentally, socially and relationally. The stagnation pathway results in a cynical view of others. Stagnant people become obstructive in teams and eventually destructive to others. As they hoard opportunity, information, credit, and riches they become embittered. Nearly every bitter, toxic person I've encountered in high-pressure work environments have the mindset Erikson described. They are takers.

But he theorizes that those who choose to find their life's work by investing in others and regenerating whatever wisdom and perspective they have obtained by coaching, teaching, mentoring and leading others are significantly more vital. This stage is the one in which the most highly effective and impactful leaders I've known live. Unbound by earlier stage-of-life struggles, these leaders tirelessly invest in the advancement of other people. They are a force of nature. It is this stage of human development that yields the most effective Supervisors.

I am not suggesting, nor is Erikson, that someone younger than 40 is unable to be an effective leader. History is full of examples of young, powerful, humble, effective leaders in their 20s, 30s and early 40s. What I am suggesting is that to be effective at a younger age means the individual has achieved the Industry, Intimacy, Independence and Self Awareness of Erikson's earlier stages.

The opposite, as you may have already thought, is also true. Just because someone is 50 does not mean he is, by default, an excellent leader. Erikson's stages of human development are built on the premise that one must successfully complete each previous stage as a prerequisite for the next one.

My point is at least this: the most effective supervisory leaders in High-Impact organizations are so comfortable with themselves that they have the mental and psychological energy to freely invest in others. They are free from the shackles of their own underdeveloped personalities. Their joy, once arising from personal accomplishment, is now exponentially greater as they pour themselves into others who ultimately succeed.

Does this describe you?

Oh, one more thing: Erickson's final stage of human development is called "Integrity vs. Despair." This stage, sometimes lasting two or three decades, is a reflective one wherein we look at our lives with either a sense of satisfaction or failure. We feel proud of our relationships, decisions, and accomplishments with few regrets and a deep sense of integrity. Or we are depressed by what we could have or should have done.

While Erikson's stages of development may be too rigid and formulaic for my taste and for the real stuff of life, they are quite instructive... even inspiring. As adults they leave us with three assignments: First, learn to grapple with the individual you are when you are alone, focusing on the type of person you want to become. Take action to become the person you would admire. Second, take what you've learned and multiply it by serving others through mentorship and coaching. Third, live outside of yourself so that you savor the joy of a regret-free life.

> **Resilient Supervisory Skill #28: Invest in others. Learn skills and develop competencies so that you can pass them along to other people. Always be coaching.**

Chapter 23:

A Bias for Action

Is there something you need to do? What came to mind? Stop. Go do it. Right now. Then come back. This is important. If it's a big thing, chop it into tiny steps and do the first, smallest thing. Go. Hit pause, and put a bookmark on the page. Go.

> **Resilient Supervisory Skill #29: Develop a Bias for Action, rather than a Bias for Delaying Until Later (for whatever reason).**

Welcome back. What you just did is a discipline practiced by highly effective leaders.[51] Especially if what you did is tied to a goal. If you thought of something, talked yourself out of it in a flash, continued reading, you missed out on one of the most simple, powerful disciplines of life.

---

51 Hi there. You just kept reading, didn't you? You probably thought of something you needed to do, but you didn't do it. In a flash, you justified not doing it. Just like that. The moment passed. You reinforced your bias for anything but acting. It's that basic. Just sayin'.

■ *Thinking about doing something is not the same thing as doing it.*

I know, rocket science, huh? Thinking about the perspectives and tools I've presented here is not the same as practicing them. The difference between highly effective Supervisors and average ones is this: *they do what they need to do when they need to do it.* They do not put things off. "Now" is their favorite word. Somewhere in life, they learned that the "right time" never arrives. So, when they see something that needs to be addressed, they act. They do not let their own intelligence and psychology weave a web of tangled excuses for not acting. They act.[52]

At a recent Supervisory summit, I presented the *Power of Expectations* tool, along with the research that suggests most Supervisors are not good at expressing clear expectations. Melanie took notes, asked questions, and nodded during this segment of the training.

When she returned from our lunch break, she had written out her expectations ensuring they were behavioral, emailed them to each member of her team and scheduled meetings to address any questions. It took her 20 minutes. She created details for the T-3 Model while I presented the idea and sent a draft copy to her fellow Supervisors for review. By the second day of the training, she had gotten feedback, made edits and scheduled performance conversations in the next month with two team members who were deficient in their performance.

Melanie has a Bias for Action.

When I asked you a few paragraphs ago if there is something you need to do, it is highly likely that you just kept reading. In less than three seconds, you talked yourself out of doing it. Maybe you will do it later. Perhaps not. This is a bias for thinking. Or a bias for feeling, especially if "I don't feel like it right now" is the primary reason you give yourself for not acting.

---

52 It might be worth rereading that paragraph. Then doing it.

Perhaps you have a Bias for Action. When I asked what you needed to do, maybe you put the book down and worked out. Or maybe you threw a load in the laundry, returned a call, wrote an email, crossed ice cream off your grocery list. Perhaps you apologized, arranged, asked or answered. If what you did is aligned with where you want to go or what you want to be, you've just demonstrated a bias for action. Congratulations. You didn't wait, analyze, psyche yourself up, plan to plan to do, check your internal emotional battery levels. You just moved. Aristotle would be proud.[53]

Let's understand it a little more so that the next time you realize action is necessary, you will act. You will have a little more of a Bias for Action.

Most of us have an assumption that knowledge brings about change. We believe we are thinkers who feel and act. When data abounds, and information is nearly free, knowledge is often obscured. Information, even in piles, does not naturally result in knowledge. Data measured, information connected, results in knowledge. Knowledge, however, isn't enough. Knowing how and when to act, knowing what to do in any given situation, is wisdom. Knowing how it all works, specifically in each situation, is wisdom.

To be frank, there are themes about which I have wisdom (data plus information plus knowledge applied in a context) that do not result in the change I desire or in the accomplishment of the goal I've set. Why?

Why, when I know what I should do and know how to do it, do I not do it? This is at the root of the broader question: Why does change not occur, even when formally and mutually agreed upon by groups?

Many of us, many of our teams and organizations, have a mental model or an assumption—a belief—that increased knowledge, especially when compellingly packaged, will result in a sustained change in

---

[53] https://plato.stanford.edu/entries/aristotle-ethics/ Aristotle wrote often of Virtuous Activity as the gateway of Virtue rather than Virtue as the gateway to doing good. Hence, Do Good, Be Good.

behavior. We hop on the change wheel at the Know More spot, hope to Feel Motivated, then through the sheer expenditure of stored energy, Act. This is a bias for knowledge.

When we try to energize ourselves through internal and external motivational tools, looking to change how we feel before acting, we demonstrate a bias for feelings. But, if your mind is racing ahead of these words, you know that those who change and sustain it, develop a Bias for Action.

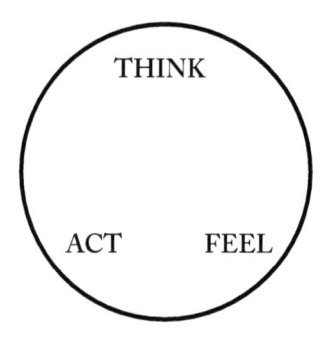

```
        THINK

   ACT       FEEL
```

Since our brain is primarily a survival system, it will neurologically and neurochemically default to the functional pathway that requires the least energy. Why run when you can walk? Why walk when you can sit? Why sit when you can lie down, or lie down when you can sleep?

Why move when you can plan to move? Why plan to move when you can think more? Why think when you can daydream? Why daydream when you can sleep? You get the idea. Action happens only if we swim upstream, as far as mental and physical energy is concerned. It is true at home, at play, and at work. Applying any of the tools I suggest will require a Bias for Action. In fact, when any change is required, when we adopt a new skill or advance an old one, we must develop a Bias for Action.

Here's another rather harsh reality: We only have a few seconds following an idea in which to act before the survival system in our brain overrides the decision system. Even when the action is something we want to accomplish, and even when it is directly related to our goals, the pauses after the idea give rise to the brain's survival instinct.

Whether in a meeting or an email, whether in a phone call or a conversation, we develop a Bias for Action as we recognize the next small step and immediately take it. If we do not take the first step toward our goal or outcome, regardless of how minor or trivial, our survival brain and supporting psychology will put the idea on an increasing heap of hopes and wishes and plans, never to be seen again. The "someday" pile buries most organizations and teams. Do it now.

> *The "I will do it later" habit creates a "someday" pile that buries most teams and organizations.*

This is particularly powerful when applied to large complex or emotionally encumbered initiatives. The work ahead seems daunting. We default to thinking, planning and hoping for the right time, a better time, the perfect moment. But if we take the first, most obvious step, regardless of how small, we will develop a Bias for Action. And the action transforms the landscape of the challenge as we do it.

As I write this chapter, I am miles above the Rockies on a flight from Seattle to Miami. The seats are comfortable and luxurious (thank you Alaska Airlines for the upgrade to first class). The Starbucks coffee is wonderfully aromatic and hot. The headphones block out a loud talker behind me. The view below is stunning. I think: *I am going to write another chapter.* I've developed a Bias for Action, so instead of staring out the window for a few more minutes (or the entire six-hour flight), I immediately reach into my European Shoulder Bag, grab my iPad Pro, open it up to this page and begin to write. The action took 20 seconds. That is a Bias for Action.

As a Supervisor, developing a Bias for Action is vital. Act. It does not need to be dramatic, sweeping, grand and strategic action. Just action. As soon as you know the next small step, take it. Move. Make the call. Write the email. Put it on your calendar. Open it. Close it. Ask the question. If you think of something to do in support of a goal, take action. Now.

A small action jump-starts the momentum of our mind and body. You are thinking of something right now that you want or need to accomplish. Here's your opportunity (again). Stop reading and act. Regardless of what you feel like, act. Now. You can come back to this page in a few minutes. [54]

Here's the fun news: This bias does not magically become easier as time goes on. We are hardwired to use the least amount of mental and physical energy at every moment. Overcoming that mental default, while not complicated, will require the same amount of focus and willpower (a limited supply) now as it will later in life. It will require the same focus with small actions as it does with large ones. While habits become easier over time, since they are invisible mental and physical processes in the background of our consciousness, this is a discipline. Disciplines are like habits, but they require a bump to get them started; a momentary act of will.

Here's the good news: The choice to act, to move, takes two seconds. Maybe three. And as the seconds pass while we ponder, action becomes increasingly difficult. Thinking ourselves into action rarely works. Just move. If it is difficult for you, even if it's very, very difficult, it will only last a few seconds. As you act, notice how much easier the action gets after a few seconds.

Once, when I was a teenager, I complained about how difficult something was to my Uncle Marv. He laughed and said it wouldn't last long then added, "Boy, you could stand on your head in a pile of hot horse manure for a minute if you needed to. So, get on with it."

---

[54] By the way, this simple discipline is also what separates intentionally effective people from accidentally effective ones. Intentionally effective people achieve excellence as a matter of course. Accidentally effective people only occasionally and then only when all the winds of weirdness blow in their favor.

Over the years, as I debate with myself in the two seconds following an impulse to act on a goal, I've found myself recalling Uncle Marv's words with a chuckle. And I move. Thankfully, life has never required standing on my head for a full minute in any substance.

Point of Leverage

Tips for developing a Bias for Action in your team:
1. At the end of every conversation, ask what the team member will do because of the conversation.
2. Ask when he will do it.
3. Listen for any action that can be taken now. Reinforce acting now.

Minimize the Change: Small Steps, Large Results

Any goal we have and any change we want to see, regardless of its scope and complexity, can be reduced to small, incremental actions. The components of a goal are all actionable. This age-old wisdom is lost on us in the Information Age. It is buried under the stampede to outsource personal responsibility afforded by the connected age. When the change we envision and truly desire does not occur, we double down by looking for more data, better information or a more reliable outsource.

> *Those who turn ideas into impact and impact into transformative change are those who have a Bias for Action.*

Regardless of how effectively our networks foster connectivity and regardless of how much we know, we will never escape the truth that those who turn ideas into impact and impact into transformative change are those who have a Bias for Action. It will never get easier (or more difficult) to act than it is right now. Action, even in its smallest form, starts the process of achievement in all forms. Whatever change you want to see in yourself, your team or in individuals on your team, shrink that change to its smallest initial behavior and act on it.

When someone says they will do something later, ask them to put it into action by putting it on the calendar now. When you think of getting an answer to a question, call the person now. When you get irritated because you forgot to pay the water bill at home, set up auto pay now.

When you are frustrated with the way a team member interacts with a customer, walk over and give the feedback now. In the middle of a team meeting, when you think of a class, you want to attend, open your calendar and put "register for class" on it for a specific date and time.

The next time you hear a friend wax eloquent about his plans... again... challenge him to take the first small step now. Immediately. Since there are no big steps in life, these small, immediate actions are pivotal. Essential even.

One more time: If you are thinking of something you want or need to do to accomplish a goal as you read or listen to this book, stop and do it now. The book will be here when you come back.

Resilient Supervisory Skill #30: Finish every Supervisory conversation with the question: What will you do now?

Chapter 24:

Conclusion

The resilient supervisory leader is not a freak of nature, an accident, or an odd combination of luck and good genetics who just happens into the job. He is intentionally resilient. He has learned to manage his assumptions, to focus on the few things in life and at work that really matter and has developed a Bias for Action.

A resilient Supervisor in a High-Impact organization is a leader who thrives under pressure, leads individuals and small groups to higher levels of performance and gets results.

Every one of the leaders with whom we have worked with believes people deserve good leadership. They are motivated by a deep, insatiable curiosity for how things really are. They have a nearly endless passion for the work before them and a buoyant, humble joy that brings a smile to the faces of their team, even in times of high stress and pressure.

I hope that you will benefit from what we have discovered through more than 30 years of study of these resilient leaders in High-Impact organizations as you take some of these ideas and turn them into action and then into habits.

The people you serve deserve good leadership.

All the best to you!

De Hicks, Ph.D., M.S., M.B.A.

Chapter 25:

The Short List of Resilient Supervisor Skills

- ☐ Skill #1: Figure out why you work.
- ☐ Skill #2: Explain what things mean by connecting the What with the Why.
- ☐ Skill #3: Practice being a Window, a Compass, and a Mirror.
- ☐ Skill #4: Whenever a change in Roles occurs, clarify in writing and in conversation the change in the other Rs of the supervisory relationship.
- ☐ Skill #5: Check your Assumptions.
- ☐ Skill #6: Whenever a conflict occurs, identify and correct the assumptions that created it.
- ☐ Skill #7: Ask, "What am I missing?"
- ☐ Skill #8: When the going gets tough, return to the fundamentals.
- ☐ Skill #9: Emphasize personal responsibility.
- ☐ Skill #10: If you see something, say something. You are the Keeper of the Culture.
- ☐ Skill #11: Connect the WHAT with the WHY. Use the "This SO THAT That" model.
- ☐ Skill #12: Remember, we do what we do because it works for us. We

change behavior (eventually) if it no longer works for us.
- ☐ Skill #13: Create and Communicate the Results each team and individual is to achieve within the next one to three months.
- ☐ Skill #14: Begin immediately describing what is changing and what is not changing during times of transition.
- ☐ Skill #15: Assign Chapter 15 as a reading assignment for your team. Create a No-Venting discipline and make it effective on a specific date.
- ☐ Skill #16: Teach your team members to take personal responsibility for communication. Take note of communication problems that occur because the information was too difficult to discover and fix those scenarios one by one.
- ☐ Skill #17: Write out three performance standards that apply to the entire team and three performance standards that apply to each individual. Communicate the standards verbally and in writing at your next team meeting. See what happens.
- ☐ **Skill #18: Practice the Power of Expectations.**
- ☐ **Skill #19: Break the Triangles and practice direct communication.**
- ☐ **Skill #20: Use the What, What, What tool this week.**
- ☐ **Skill #21: Practice using the SLY approach to problem-solving.**
- ☐ Skill #22: Practice Tipping the conversation back to the issue at hand whenever someone becomes distracted by other seemingly related problems.
- ☐ Skill #23: Practice separating Observed Behavior from what you think the behavior means.
- ☐ Skill #24: Do it now.
- ☐ Skill #25: Use your Calendar for Everything. Decide how you will use your time well before you use it.
- ☐ Skill #26: Become a Pro and expect Professionalism out of your Team Members using the T-3 Model
- ☐ Skill #27: Manage your vitality every day, without fail, for the rest of your life.
- ☐ Skill #28: Invest in others. Learn skills and develop competencies so

THE SHORT LIST OF RESILIENT SUPERVISOR SKILLS

that you can pass them along to other people. Always be coaching.
- ☐ Skill #29: Develop a Bias for Action, rather than a Bias for Delaying Until Later (for whatever reason).
- ☐ Skill #30: Finish every Supervisory conversation with the question: What will you do now?

About the Author

De Hicks is the Founder and President of the RMC Group of Companies. SCGI is the oldest of those companies, specializing in research-based solutions to the complex challenges High-Impact leaders face.

Dr. Hicks has supported and learned from leaders for over three decades, as they grow their organizations while contending with massive economic, cultural, technological and professional challenges.

"Adventure over comfort" is the guiding principle of his life. An avid lover of the motorcycle lifestyle, De is more often on a bike taking a long way around, regardless of wind and weather, than in a car.

While parents never admit to having favorites among their children,

De's favorite company is undoubtedly Rottweiler Motorcycle Company, Inc. A family adventure started in the fall of 2006, RMC has become a vital contributor to the motorcycle enthusiast culture and attracts riders far and wide.

For more about Dr. Hicks, to see his books and podcasts, or to get in touch, go to www.dehicks.com.

INDEX

A

accidental 78, 80, 113
acting supervisor .. 28, 29, 124, 168, 170, 173
adjustment disorder 69, 70
ambiguity 54
Amos Tversky 53
asking questions 41
assume ..38, 39, 46, 48, 53, 71, 92, 139, 153
assumptions ... 2, 7, 13, 37, 38, 39, 40, 41, 42, 43, 46, 47, 48, 49, 50, 52, 54, 55, 56, 77, 86, 87, 88, 92, 160, 175
authority 36

B

Becoming a Supervisor 23

behavior 6, 16, 18, 19, 20, 21, 43, 68, 73, 74, 75, 80, 82, 85, 93, 94, 95, 121, 125, 126, 127, 134, 135, 136, 137, 138, 140, 143, 174
Behavioral Economics 53
brain 35, 36, 46, 47, 48, 49, 50, 54, 55, 56, 60, 61, 70, 115, 129, 136, 138, 170, 171

C

calendar 31, 62, 95, 96, 139, 145, 146, 147, 172, 174
Calendar 145, 149, 178
change 105
change wheel 170
coach 30, 55, 85
community oriented 67
compass 17, 18, 84
complaining 45, 75, 121

INDEX

complexity....11, 35, 38, 50, 54, 173
conflict........ 24, 31, 36, 37, 43, 46, 74, 76, 92, 93, 94, 95, 116, 117, 157, 160, 161
Connectivity 2, 65, 67, 69, 71, 72
Consequence 136, 137
consistency.......38, 84, 88, 89, 117
Consistency 85, 89
continual learning..................... 6
conversation.......................... 109
crucial conversations 43
culture...65, 72, 77, 78, 79, 80, 81, 82, 111, 112, 113, 128, 182
Culture 77, 78, 80, 81, 111
curiosity ..2, 41, 45, 49, 51, 55, 57, 92, 141, 175

D

Daniel Kahneman 53
Decision Fatigue...................... 61
diet .. 53, 79, 134, 157, 158, 159, 161
Dog Whistle of Leadership 45
drama... 63, 72, 89, 109, 112, 113, 128, 138, 160, 161
dynamic expert 42, 154

E

Eisenhower Method Urgent, Important 30
emotional 46, 84, 92, 93, 104, 124, 160, 169

exercise ... 47, 50, 134, 148, 157, 159
Expectations 20, 119, 122, 168

F

Finalization 66
Five Rs of Leadership............. 27
friendship 17, 31
frustration............................. 109

G

glucose 54
goal
goals; goal system.............. 35, 36, 71, 117, 142, 143, 167, 169, 171, 172, 173, 174
Goals 115, 142

H

habit 109
habit system...33, 35, 36, 55, 60, 94, 95, 125, 127, 162
halo effect 53, 54
health...............79, 157, 159, 160
High Impact Organization........ 5

I

innovate 5
Insight 53, 147
intentions...........................46, 95

184

interest 2, 8, 32
Interpretation 136, 137, 138
interruptions 30, 37, 60

K

Keeper of the Culture 30

L

landlines 66
lead Supervisor .. 6, 27, 28, 29, 39, 47, 49, 52, 55, 88, 113, 142, 154
Leverage 7, 8, 40
leveraged 6, 7, 29, 40, 95
Listen 13, 45, 57, 135, 173
low entertainment-to-education consumption ratio 159

M

mature friendships 32
Measurements 116
mental models 3, 7, 36, 37, 39, 40, 41, 42, 45, 46, 47, 49, 50, 54, 57, 67, 126
metabolic rate 158
micro-manage 140
mirror 17, 19, 20, 92
mission 11, 13, 18, 68, 73, 80, 85, 103, 116, 144
motivation 20, 54
Multi-tasking 49, 60

N

networks 66, 68, 69, 173
neuropsychological 54
neuropsychology 52
norms 78, 79, 80, 81, 82, 131

O

observe 31, 37, 38, 46, 137, 138
Observed Behavior 136, 138
OIC Model of communication 136
outsourcing of personal responsibility 68

P

pattern 20, 50, 51, 92, 140
peer 28, 29, 32
Performance 16, 62, 115, 116, 117, 119, 125, 129, 130, 135, 136, 140
Performance Improvement 16
Performance Standards 115, 116
personal responsibility ... 66, 68, 72, 74, 75, 103, 173
Point of Leverage 7, 9, 10, 13, 14, 16, 17, 20, 33, 35, 40, 43, 45, 57, 82, 90, 104, 130, 173, 179
Power of Assumptions
Assumptions 35, 38, 48
Principle of One 146

INDEX

promoted from within 25

Q

quality 30, 60, 72, 121
questions 23, 24, 43, 55, 56, 95, 129, 130, 168

R

Relationships 15, 27, 28, 31, 33
resilience 41, 92
Resilient .. 6, 11, 54, 59, 61, 85, 115, 157, 158
Resilient Supervisors .. 6, 11, 59, 85, 158
Resources 27, 28, 32, 33
respect 36, 42, 124
Responsibilities 27, 28, 33
results 1, 6, 7, 8, 11, 13, 16, 17, 20, 27, 48, 56, 65, 77, 95, 104, 109, 113, 128, 169
Results 173
reticular activating system 37
Richard Thaler 53
Role 27, 28, 29, 30, 33
ROWE 97, 98
Rule of One 60
Rules of Engagement ... 27, 28, 29, 30, 31, 33

S

Saturation 66, 67
shift work 158
sleep 9, 39, 112, 134, 146, 157, 158, 159, 161, 170
sleep study 158
smart phone 66
social media 69
Spam 79, 80, 81
standard 72, 80, 112, 115, 116, 117, 136, 142, 143
Static experts 42, 153
stewardship 149
superpower 37, 50, 51, 55
Supervisory team 8, 24

T

T-3 Model of Professionalism. 154
team 107
track your time 148

U

unintended consequence 75

V

values 19, 50, 77, 78, 83, 92, 93, 116, 124

Venting 108, 109
vision 6, 116

W

will power 61, 172
window 17, 18, 54, 137, 171
workplace culture 7, 77
worry 62, 159

About the Archimedes Experiment

Founded in 2000 by Dr. Hicks, the Archimedes Experiment is an enterprise focused on the practical application of research that seeks to shed light on the leveraged behaviors, mental models and habits of High-Impact Leaders and Influencers across many professions. The findings of our research are distilled into practical and fundamental behaviors that, if replicated, result in sustained effectiveness.

For more about the Archimedes Experiment, go to www.ArchimedesExperiment.com.

Made in the USA
Middletown, DE
12 September 2020